ACKNOWLEDGEMENTS

I would like to thank the following people for their help:

Roger Arnold, David Burrill, John Chalcraft, Paul Chancellor, Peter Crangle, D.J. Dippie, John Law, Michael Mercer, Hugh Parkin, Bill Reed, Andrew Warnes, Sue Warnes, Tony Watson, David P. Williams.

Special thanks are due to my son Tristram for his help and encouragement throughout the project.

Photographs from author's collection unless otherwise stated.

Great Northern Books Limited
PO Box 1380, Bradford, BD5 5FB
www.greatnorthernbooks.co.uk

ISBN: 978-1-914227-53-0

Design and layout: David Burrill

CIP Data
A catalogue for this book is available from the British Library

INTRODUCTION

Sir William A. Stanier's 'Jubilee' 5XP 4-6-0 Class served as the backbone of passenger services for the London Midland & Scottish Railway – as well as the successor London Midland Region – for a number of years. Despite initial design flaws, the class went on to be well-liked by enginemen and enthusiasts alike. Four locomotives were preserved following withdrawal near the end of steam and continue to remind the public of their past heyday.

The London Midland & Scottish Railway was formed by the Grouping of 1923, becoming the largest of the 'Big Four' railway companies produced by this event. The LMSR's territory covered the West Midlands, North West, parts of Scotland and lines into Wales. There were many passenger duties, ranging from short inter-city trains to long-distance and cross-country services.

Despite the size of company, the locomotive classes available for these duties were not particularly strong. The London & North Western Railway contributed 'Claughton' Class 4-6-0s which had steaming troubles and 'Prince of Wales' 4-6-0s with a low power rating. The Midland Railway favoured the use of 2P and 4P Class 4-4-0s with modest loads and employed pairs of engines on heavier services, with a similar policy in use by the Caledonian Railway.

George Hughes of the Lancashire & Yorkshire Railway was the first Chief Mechanical Engineer of the LMSR, yet he retired after two years in the role and was replaced by his assistant Henry Fowler. The latter had been with the Midland Railway before Grouping and continued to promote his previous company's policy for passenger services. Large numbers of 4-4-0s were constructed in the late 1920s and early 1930s, though a small step towards better locomotives was made in 1927. Fowler was induced to build a 4-6-0 following a successful trial of a Great Western Railway 'Castle' Class 4-6-0 designed by Charles Collett. Fifty 'Royal Scot' 4-6-0s were ordered from the North British Locomotive Company and 20 appeared from Derby Works. All these were initially sent to ex-LNWR sheds mainly for West Coast Main Line duties, with several long runs necessary. Coal consumption became a problem, but this was soon traced to faults with the piston rings and a resolution had a dramatic reduction in fuel use, leaving the Royal Scots as capable engines. Some of the LNWR's Claughton Class were later rebuilt as 'Patriot' Class 4-6-0s on similar lines to the Royal Scots.

Fowler retired in the early 1930s and following a spell with an interim CME (Ernest Lemon), William Stanier was appointed on 1st January 1932. He started his career at Swindon for the GWR and held several positions under G.J. Churchward and Charles Collet, being influenced by their simple, robust designs that were well maintained to provide reliable, high-performing locomotives. Whilst Stanier's first design was the 'Princess Royal' Pacific, he soon had to meet the need for express and mixed traffic 4-6-0s which had a wide route availability. With his background away from the LMSR and constituents, Stanier was able to improve many areas of previous design practice, including axleboxes, springs, cylinders, firebox and cab. The new 5XP Class 4-6-0 was authorised during mid-1932 and included in the 1934 building programme. Fifty-eight to be erected at Crewe and Derby were part of this initially, though the plans soon evolved and another 50 were ordered from the North British Locomotive Company at the end of the year. The latter was expected to supply all in time for the summer season, but the delivery eventually proved protracted. Orders for another 83 engines took the class total to 191 by the end of 1936.

Swindon practice promoted the use of a relatively small number of superheater tubes in the boiler and this worked satisfactorily for the GWR over a number of years. Stanier used this principle in his first boilers and soon found the conditions of the LMSR called for a greater degree of superheat to have the best performance from the boiler. Around a dozen different variations were tried over the first few years from the Jubilee's introduction before the final design was settled on. The initial boilers had a straight throatplate with a 14-element superheater and the latter subsequently increased to 21-elements. Starting from no. 5665, a sloping throatplate firebox was introduced, giving a grate area of 31 sq. ft (compared with 29.5 sq. ft of the straight throatplate). The number of elements started at 21, though towards the end of the construction cycle, 24 elements became standard and this was true for all Jubilee boilers post-war. Also, the first boilers had smokebox regulators, but dome-mounted regulators later replaced this arrangement. An equally important change was made to the size of the blastpipe cap and the position of this in the smokebox. The original cap was wide with bars incorporated and placed quite close to the boiler centre line. When the blastpipe diameter was reduced and free from obstruction, as well as lowered by many inches, the draughting improved as did the performance.

As the modified boilers came into use, confidence in the class increased and the locomotives settled to their work. In the first six months from their introduction in 1934, 90 had been constructed and mainly found homes at ex-LNWR sheds on the WCML. A small number found their way to former Midland establishments at Bristol and Leeds, though the balance had changed as 1935 drew to a close with 130 Jubilees in service. The ex-MR shed at Kentish Town received the bulk, followed by Holbeck, whilst Sheffield, Derby and Nottingham depots began their associations with the class. For Scottish services, Carlisle Kingmoor had the most 5XPs, though Aberdeen and Perth had engines for a time. Corkerhill shed, Glasgow, later became the main Scottish shed for the Jubilees.

The first Jubilees initially had Fowler-style 3,500-gallon tenders with a coal space carrying 7 tons of coal. Then, the NBLC-built locomotives appeared with new Stanier 4,000-gallon tenders capable of holding 9 tons of coal, whilst a third type was the slightly smaller Stanier 3,500-gallon tender with 7 tons of coal which was paired with nos 5617-5666. During the construction period, the Royal Scot Class was given priority over new build 4,000-gallon tenders being built with nos 5695-5725 and these received the Royal Scots' Fowler 3,500-gallon tenders. NBLC-built engines were also nominated to relinquish their higher capacity tenders between 1935 and 1937. The exchanges were soon seen to be disadvantageous to the Jubilees and from 1937 to 1940, 4F Class 0-6-0s were built with 4,000-gallon tenders to replace those lost. Towards the late 1950s, a final push to remove the Fowler 3,500-gallon tenders was made and around 40 Jubilees took Stanier 4,000-gallon tenders from 8F Class 2-8-0s.

The Jubilee Class began their career in the LMSR's Crimson Lake passenger livery with Derby scroll typeface used on the smokebox number plate and cab-side numerals, along with the company branding on the tender. From around mid-1936, the style for new engines changed to Sans Serif and was also recorded on a small number of older locomotives. This was later discontinued and the Jubilees went into the Second World War where they mostly lost their colour for a plain black livery. Around 30 are known to have retained Crimson Lake and a locomotive had an experimental livery in red following the end of the conflict, as well as an engine in grey. Yet, gloss black with red and pale-yellow lining was chosen as the standard for the near future during 1946. Around 50 Jubilees were affected up to the formation of British Railways in 1948. For a time, a version of the black livery was favoured before the adoption of BR's Brunswick green with orange and black lining was chosen for express locomotives and first applied in the latter half of 1949. This mainly saw the class to withdrawal in the mid-to late 1960s, though there were instances of unlined green in the last days of steam. BR favoured Gill Sans type for numbers and later cab numbers, though there were variations and the company's name initially adorned the tenders of locomotives. This was superseded by an emblem in the early 1950s, followed by a grant of arms in 1957.

Initially, the Jubilee Class was just referred to as Class 5XP engines and ran without names. George V's Silver Jubilee year occurred six months after the introduction of the locomotives and the pageantry associated with this event informed schemes to promote and name the class. The first class member, no. 5552, still had the original boiler in early 1935, so one of the newer locomotives, no. 5462 switched identities to become no. 5552 *Silver Jubilee*. Additionally, the engine was specially treated to wear gloss black livery with chrome trim to the boiler, cab numbers and tender branding. A short time elapsed before the other locomotives were christened. Several themes were ultimately used, but the principal ones were British Empire and the Royal Navy – both admirals and ships – with a small number of previously used names from old engines also applied.

The first Jubilee Class to be condemned was no. 45637 *Windward Islands* which was involved with the Harrow & Wealdstone disaster in 1952 and damaged beyond repair. The next occurred in 1960 with a solitary locomotive, followed by three in 1961 and 1962 saw over forty removed from service. The worst year for the Jubilees was 1964 with 64 class members lost. The first to be preserved was no. 45596 *Bahamas* in 1966 following purchase by the Bahamas Locomotive Society. In 1967 just eight class members remained but all had left traffic by the end of the year. No. 45593 *Kolhapur* became the second Jubilee to be saved early in 1968. Another two were ultimately reprieved from the cutter's torch. No. 45690 *Leander* was bought from the Woodham Brothers scrapyard in 1972 and subsequently restored, whilst no. 45699 *Galatea* left the same location in 1980, originally for spares but was later also returned to working order.

At the time of writing, no. 45596 and no. 45699 have long-term boiler certificates, whilst no. 45690's is due to expire at the end of 2023. No. 45593 is currently awaiting a refurbishment which will return the locomotive to the main line once more. With the Jubilee Class relatively well represented still, hopefully they will continue to be so and honour their fallen class mates, many of which are remembered here in this collection spanning their lifetime, 1934-1967.

Peter Tuffrey
Doncaster, April 2023

London Midland & Scottish Railway

Above NO. 5552 – NOTTINGHAM MIDLAND STATION

In 1935, George V had been on the throne for 25 years and a number of commemorations of the event occurred. Jubilee Class no. 5642 was redecorated in gloss black livery with chrome highlights in April 1935, switching identities with the first class member, no. 5552, in the process. The engine was also named *Silver Jubilee*. This provided the LMSR with the official name for the 5XP designated engines – Jubilee Class. During the summer of 1935, no. 5552 *Silver Jubilee* travelled across the system to promote the company and has reached Nottingham Midland station in this image. Photograph by T.G. Hepburn from Rail Archive Stephenson courtesy Rail-Online.

Below NO. 5554 – CREWE STATION

The first five Stanier Jubilees built at Crewe Works appeared in May/June 1934 and took numbers 5552-6. No. 5554 was completed early in June and was new to Preston, though later in the summer transferred to Bushbury. At the start of 1935, the locomotive began the first of four years at Rugby. During this period, no. 5554 has been caught alongside a platform at Crewe station. The engine was christened *Ontario* in March 1936. Photograph by W.H. Whitworth from Rail Archive Stephenson courtesy Rail-Online.

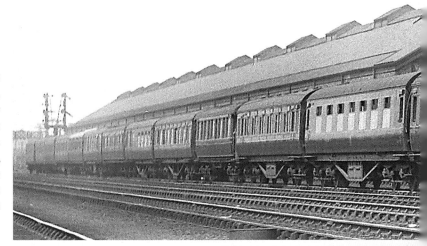

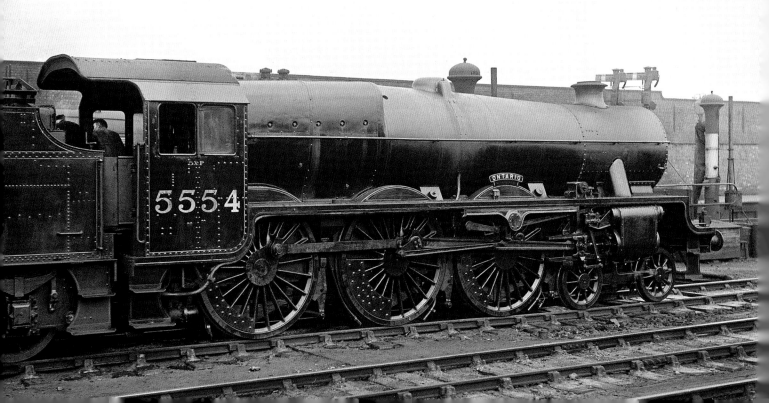

Above NO. 5553 – CREWE

Southbound at Crewe in the late 1930s is no. 5553 *Canada*. The locomotive was the second Jubilee in traffic at the end of May 1934. A feature of the first five class members was a bogie wheelbase of 6 ft 3 in. whereas subsequent engines had this measurement 3 in. longer. Another trait of the quintet was a Fowler-type tender which carried 7 tons of coal and had a 3,500-gallon water capacity. Initially allocated to Camden depot, no. 5553 soon moved northward to Preston and was at several other locations before settling at Rugby in late 1935. The locomotive was named *Canada* during February 1937. Photograph by W.H. Whitworth from Rail Archive Stephenson courtesy Rail-Online.

Above NO. 5556 – LICHFIELD TRENT VALLEY STATION

An express speeds through Lichfield Trent Valley station behind no. 5556 *Nova Scotia* when the engine was nearly new in 1934/1935. Photograph from Rail Archive Stephenson courtesy Rail-Online.

Below NO. 5560 – CREWE WORKS

Of the 50 Jubilees ordered from the North British Locomotive Company, half were built at Hyde Park Works and half came from Queen's Park Works. No. 5560 was the product of the first mentioned in July 1934 and is pictured at Crewe Works on the 22nd of that month. Photograph by Les Hanson from the David Hanson Archive courtesy Rail-Online.

Above NO. 5563 – CAMDEN SHED

Between duties during September 1938, no. 5563 *Australia* is in the shed yard at Camden. Despite being a main line shed, Camden often had periods without Jubilees. No. 5563 was visiting from Longsight, Manchester, at the time. Photograph by Colling Turner from Rail Archive Stephenson courtesy Rail-Online.

Below NO. 5570

No. 5570 *New Zealand* stands outside an unidentified shed with modified domed boiler. The engine was new from the NBLC in August 1934 with domeless boiler. Photograph by P.J. Hughes courtesy Colour-Rail.

Above NO. 5575 – COLWICH STATION

Situated between Rugeley and Stafford on the line from Rugby, Colwich station opened on 15th September 1847 under the London & North Western Railway, though the original company was the Trent Valley Railway before amalgamation. North of the station, three lines diverged: North Staffordshire Railway to Stone; Stafford avoiding line to Norton Bridge; Stafford line. No. 5575 *Madras* is passing through Colwich station in the mid-1930s. The name is yet to be fitted, though was present from November 1937. Colwich station saw services reduced immediately post-Nationalisation and finally withdrawn in 1958. Photograph courtesy Rail-Online.

Opposite above NO. 5572 – CARLISLE UPPERBY SHED

For a brief period, Ireland was a dominion of the British Empire as a result of the Anglo-Irish Treaty of 1921 which came at the end of the Irish War of Independence. The country was known as the Irish Free State from 1922 until 1937. Jubilee no. 5572 was named *Irish Free State* in late March 1936 before the new constitution formed Ireland, or Eire, on 29th December 1937. Interestingly, the locomotive took the Gaelic name of the country – *Eire* – rather than the English when the plates were altered during July 1938. The engine was new in September 1934 and for much of the following three years worked from Carlisle Upperby, possessing the shed's '12B' code on the smokebox door in the yard, around 1937. Photograph courtesy Rail-Online.

Opposite below NO. 5573 – CREWE STATION

Black became the standard livery for locomotives during the Second World War. In 1946 some experiments into alternative schemes took place. Initially, this concerned the lining rather than the colour, yet soon afterwards no. 5573 *Newfoundland* was returned to traffic wearing a slate grey with muted lining and narrow gaps between company letters on the tender. A gloss black with red and pale-yellow lining was also trialled. No. 5573 was repainted in the last mentioned, which became standard for a time, during August 1947 and has this in the image opposite from the same year. The locomotive is light engine at Crewe station. Photograph courtesy Rail-Online.

Above **NO. 5594 – YORK**

Before no. 5573 *Newfoundland* had the experimental grey livery applied, no. 5594 *Bhopal* was returned to the pre-war Crimson Lake passenger livery. Whilst the colour was the same, the lining was slightly different and omitted completely from the cab on the driver's side. The number was placed just above the running plate and in line with the LMS on the tender. The latter was also positioned slightly closer together than previously. No. 5594 ran in this guise until 1952 when British Railways' green was applied. The engine is seen around Nationalisation with an express travelling away from York. Photograph by Ernest Sanderson courtesy Colour-Rail.

Opposite above **NO. 5587 – BROCK WATER TROUGHS**

Around seven miles north of Preston, no. 5587 *Baroda* is the pilot for another Jubilee, no. 5652 *Hawke*, which is coupled to the Royal train travelling over Brock water troughs in 1937. The London & North Western Railway built two luxurious new carriages for King Edward VII and Queen Alexandra following their accession to the throne in the early 20th century. Along with several other carriages, these King and Queen saloons formed the basis of the Royal train for the West Coast through to the start of the Second World War. At this time, the set was considered too vulnerable to enemy attack and new armour-plated stock was built by the LMSR in 1941. The King and Queen saloons were later preserved as part of the National Collection. Brock water troughs were 560 yards long and installed in the 1860s. Photograph courtesy Rail-Online.

Opposite below **NO. 5591 – RUGBY**

In the late 1930s, a local train is in the Rugby area with no. 5591 *Udaipur*. The locomotive was in traffic from December 1934 after delivery from the NBLC's Queen's Park Works. Following several early moves, no. 5591 settled at Rugby in October 1935 and the allocation lasted seven years. Originally built with a Stanier 4,000-gallon tender, no. 5591 has switched to a Fowler 3,500-gallon tender obtained from Royal Scot Class 4-6-0 no. 6126 *Royal Army Service Corps*. Photograph courtesy Rail-Online.

Above NO. 5596 – OXENHOLME

Northbound at Oxenholme with a Liverpool to Glasgow express in the summer of 1935 is no. 5596. The engine was new from the NBLC's Queen's Park Works at the end of 1934 and was briefly based in Glasgow between January and March 1935. Preston's '10B' code is now on the smokebox door and this took no. 5596 into 1936. In June of that year, the locomotive was named *Bahamas*. Photograph by F.R. Hebron from Rail Archive Stephenson courtesy Rail-Online.

Below NO. 5599 – CREWE NORTH SHED

The Tswana people were under threat from South African expansionists in the early 1880s. John Mackenzie – a Scottish missionary – alerted the British Government which dispatched an armed force. This was in place when the area was proclaimed a British Protectorate in March 1885. Bechuanaland, split into two parts, was under British rule until independence occurred in 1966, becoming Botswana. As part of the naming policy for the Jubilee Class, no. 5599 was christened *Bechuanaland* during July 1936. The name had been carried for 11 years when the locomotive was pictured at Crewe North shed following a recent overhaul on 20th April 1947. No. 5599 has the gloss black livery shining and this lasted with the engine until 1952 when BR green was applied. Officially allocated to Crewe North from 26th April, the locomotive had been at Bushbury previously and moved on to Carlisle Upperby in August. Photograph courtesy Rail Photoprints.

NO. 5601 – RUNCORN

Travelling southward through Runcorn, no. 5601 *British Guiana* is piloting an unidentified Royal Scot around Nationalisation. Photograph by R.A. Whitfield courtesy Rail Photoprints.

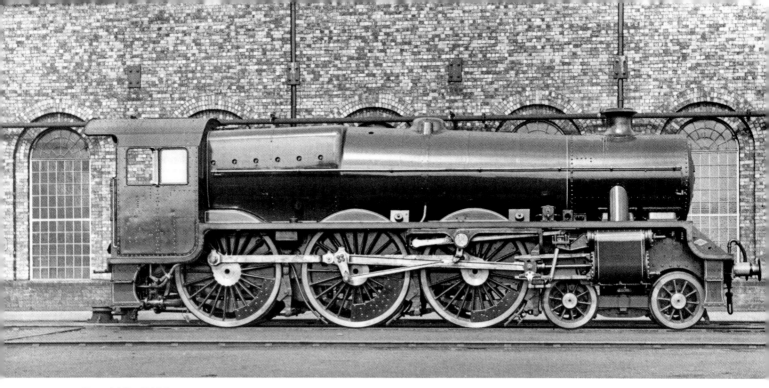

Above NO. 5603

At an unidentified location, no. 5603 appears either to be new or under repair, suggesting one of the workshops. The engine was new from the NBLC's Queen's Park Works in January 1935. On the front frame below the smokebox is the shop's diamond-shaped works plate, whilst Hyde Park had a circular plate.

Below NO. 5613 – CRICKLEWOOD SHED

On 29th May 1937 no. 5613 *Kenya* is at Cricklewood shed. Photograph courtesy Rail Photoprints.

NO. 5619 – BROCK
A short train featuring tank wagons passes over Brock water troughs in 1938 with no. 5619 *Nigeria*. Photograph courtesy Rail Photoprints.

Above NO. 5623 – LICHFIELD TRENT VALLEY STATION

Produced at Crewe Works in October 1934, no. 5623 was named *Palestine* in January 1936. The engine is at Lichfield Trent Valley station with an express in the late 1930s. Photograph courtesy Rail-Online.

Below NO. 5626

An interesting view of two Jubilee tender types together with no. 5626 *Seychelles*. A number of Fowler 3,500-gallon tenders were coupled to engines, as were Stanier's 3,500-gallon version. Yet, the Stanier 4,000-gallon tenders were favoured by the authorities and several schemes were devised over the years to reduce the number of Fowler tenders in use.

Above NO. 5629 – BRISTOL BARROW ROAD SHED

A small number of Jubilees worked from the ex-Midland Railway shed at Bristol. These were mainly employed on cross-country trains. No. 5629 *Straits Settlements* was there from summer 1939 until 1947. Photograph courtesy Colour-Rail.

Below NO. 5632 – LANCASTER

Milk tankers were developed in the 1920s/1930s as an alternative to milk churns transported in wagons. No. 5632 *Tonga* has a train featuring the tankers near Lancaster. Photograph courtesy Colour-Rail.

Above NO. 5634 – WATFORD JUNCTION

A station was built at Watford in 1837 as part of the London & Birmingham Railway. The facilities were later moved for the construction of the St Albans branch, reopening as Watford Junction in 1858. No. 5634 *Trinidad* has a Northampton train approaching there in the mid-1930s. Photograph from the Dave Cobbe Collection courtesy Rail Photoprints.

Below NO. 5633 – CREWE WORKS

No. 5633 was named *Trans-Jordan* in March 1936, then renamed *Aden* in September 1946. The engine is at Crewe Works with plates covered before a ceremony occurred at Euston. Photograph courtesy Colour-Rail.

Above NO. 5635 – CRICKLEWOOD SHED

Derby-based no. 5635 has been serviced at Cricklewood shed on 24th July 1937 after working southward. Around another month elapsed before a transfer from Derby to Liverpool Edge Hill occurred and this allocation lasted for two years. No. 5635 had been named in June 1936 at Derby Works. Photograph courtesy Rail Photoprints.

Opposite NO. 5638 – CATHIRON

Around three miles north of Rugby, the main line passed through the village of Cathiron. With two roads crossing over, there were vantage points for enthusiasts to record events over the years. On 25th May 1939, no. 5638 *Zanzibar* is viewed from Cathiron Lane travelling southward with a mixed train. Around three months earlier, the locomotive had returned to traffic following an overhaul which saw the improved boiler fitted. When pictured, no. 5638 was on the roster at Crewe North depot. Photograph from the David P. Williams Coloured Monochrome Archive.

Above **NO. 5647**

In October 1947, no. 5647 *Sturdee* received the 1946 livery and this was present to February 1951. The application looks relatively fresh here at an unidentified location. The engine was at Crewe North from April 1947 to June 1948 when a switch to Camden took place. Photograph courtesy Rail Photoprints.

Opposite above **NO. 5644 – ABERDEEN STATION**

At the end of 1935, ten Jubilees were in the Northern Division, which comprised sheds in Scotland – Aberdeen and Perth, in this instance – as well as Carlisle Kingmoor. No. 5644 *Howe* was amongst this group and allocated to Aberdeen from late 1935 to 1939 when moving on to Kingmoor. In the following year, the locomotive began the first of ten years working from Glasgow Corkerhill. Duties there included Glasgow-Aberdeen trains and Glasgow-Carlisle services. No. 5644 has one of the aforementioned at Aberdeen in 1947. Photograph courtesy Rail Photoprints.

Opposite below **NO. 5652**

When the names associated with the British Empire had been used up, the policy switched to the Royal Navy, particularly historical names. No. 5652 took *Hawke* in early June 1937 after Edward Hawke who rose through the ranks in the 18th century to become an Admiral of the Fleet and was First Lord of the Admiralty, 1766-1771. The locomotive is at an unidentified location here before naming was carried out. No. 5652 was erected at Crewe Works in January 1935 and worked from several locations between then and naming.

NO. 5655 – NOTTINGHAM STATION

New from Derby in late 1934, no. 5655 is at Nottingham station between duties in 1935. Photograph by T.G. Hepburn from Rail Archive Stephenson courtesy Rail-Online.

Above NO. 5657 – DORE AND TOTLEY
At Dore and Totley (south of Sheffield), no. 5657 *Tyrwhitt* has an express in 1938. Photograph courtesy Rail-Online.

Below NO. 5662 – MILLHOUSES
Another express in the Sheffield area at Millhouses (north of Dore and Totley), no. 5662 *Kempenfelt* (before naming) is southbound in the mid-1930s. Photograph courtesy Rail-Online.

Above NO. 5671 – CREWE WORKS

No. 5671 *Prince Rupert* was part of an experiment into ash ejection from the smokebox, the apparatus for which is visible at the top near the chimney. Recently discharged from Crewe Works in 1946, no. 5671 was equipped to the end of the decade. Photograph courtesy Rail Photoprints.

Opposite above NO. 5677 – BUSHEY

Water is taken from the troughs at Bushey (south of Watford) by no. 5677 *Beatty* in the late 1930s.

Opposite below NO. 5671 – FARNLEY JUNCTION SHED

From November 1947 to September 1948, no. 5671 *Prince Rupert* was a resident of Farnley Junction shed, Leeds. The engine is in the yard during that period. Photograph courtesy *Yorkshire Post Newspapers*.

Above NO. 5691 – WATFORD

Passing milepost 17 on the West Coast Main Line, no. 5691 *Orion* is approaching Watford with an express in 1939. Nearby, the branch to Rickmansworth departed westward. Opened in 1860, this was part of a broader plan by Baron Ebury to connect with the Great Western Railway at Uxbridge. The company later pulled out of the original arrangement and the line terminated at Rickmansworth. This was later closed in 1952. No. 5691 was Crewe-allocated in 1939 and had been from new in March 1936. In January 1941, the locomotive started the first of 13 years at Glasgow Polmadie depot.

Opposite above NO. 5685

In comparison with other Jubilee class members, no. 5685 *Barfleur* had a settled working life. Spending the first 20 months at Crewe North, the locomotive moved to Kentish Town in September 1937 and was there for the next decade. Just before Nationalisation no. 5685 made a final transfer to Bristol Barrow Road and this lasted to withdrawal in April 1964. The depot's code is on the smokebox door here. Photograph courtesy Colour-Rail.

Opposite below NO. 5693 – WATFORD

In the early 20th century, the London & North Western Railway developed an excursion service from the North and Midlands to reach the resorts on the South Coast of England. The main draw for the train was that changes were not necessary in London and engines switched at Willesden before skirting round the Capital. This 'Sunny South' express ran successfully up to the First World War, then again in the 1920s and 1930s. Returning after the Second World War, the express was unnamed from this time. No. 5693 *Agamemnon* has a northbound 'Sunny South' express at Watford on 10th June 1939. Photograph by George C. Lander courtesy Rail Photoprints.

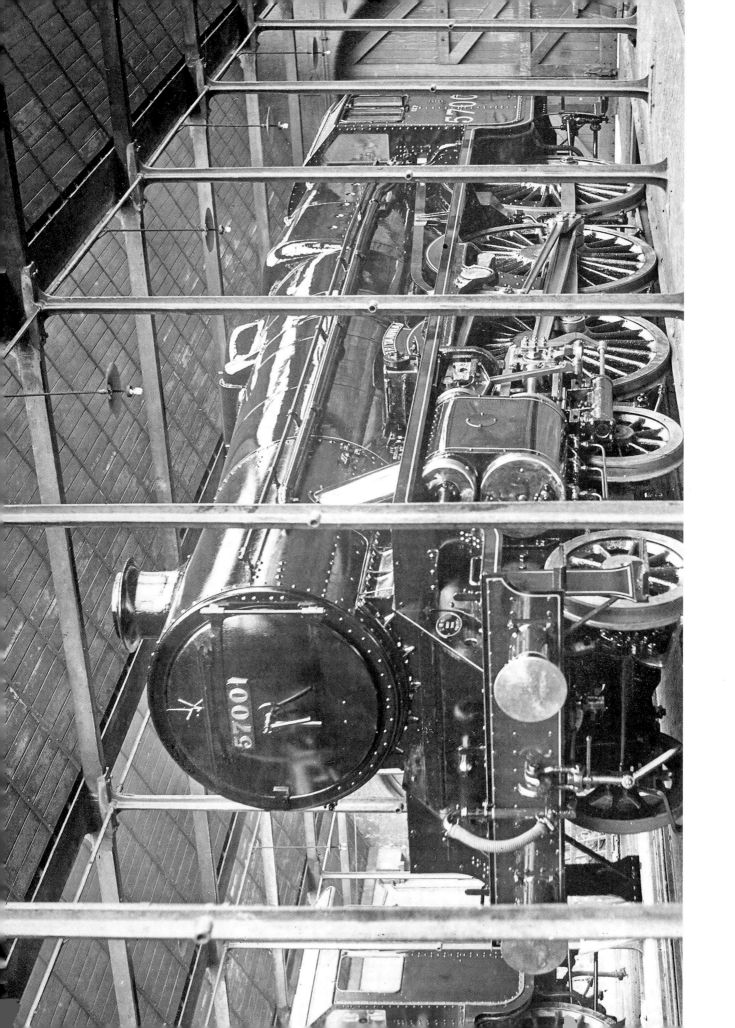

Above NO. 5701 – FARNLEY JUNCTION SHED

Newton Heath's no. 5701 *Conqueror* has reached Farnley Junction shed for servicing around Nationalisation. Interestingly, just two of the Jubilee Class had one allocation over their career. No. 5701 was associated with Newton Heath from April 1936 to February 1963, whilst no. 5658 *Keyes* worked from Leeds Holbeck from December 1934 to September 1965. Photograph courtesy *Yorkshire Post Newspapers*.

Opposite NO. 5700 – CREWE WORKS

No. 5700 *Britannia* is in the Paint Shop at Crewe Works during April 1936 when newly built. Wearing the standard Crimson Lake livery, the engine is yet to be paired with a tender. Initially with a standard Stanier 4,000-gallon example, no. 5700 entered service with tender no. 3913 from no. 6132 *The King's Regiment Liverpool* as part of the Royal Scot Class tender exchanges. No. 5700 was new to Newton Heath depot and enjoyed employment there until March 1963, with just a month on loan at Blackpool in September 1957 breaking this span. Photograph courtesy Rail-Online.

Above NO. 45556 – CAMDEN

Northbound from Euston terminus, no. 45556 *Nova Scotia* has a Manchester express on Camden incline during early June 1962. The climb was quite demanding for locomotives as gradients of 1 in 70, 1 in 112 and 1 in 77 were present for around a mile to Camden. No. 45556 survived until September 1964 and for the last decade in service had employment at Crewe shed. Photograph from the Dave Cobbe Collection courtesy Rail Photoprints.

Below NO. 45554 – SUTTON WEAVER

The Grand Junction Railway originally joined the Liverpool & Manchester Railway near Warrington, allowing access to the two cities. Shortly afterwards, a plan to shorten the route to Liverpool was formulated by running via Runcorn and crossing the River Mersey to rejoin the L&MR. The LNWR was founded before the GJR could follow through with this and the project did not reach completion until the late 1860s. The Liverpool branch left the main line at Weaver Junction and ran near the village of Sutton Weaver, which is the location for this image captured in April 1959 with no. 45554 *Ontario* passing by at the head of a southbound express. Based at Liverpool Edge Hill at this time, no. 45554 moved to Crewe in 1961 and was withdrawn there during 1964. Photograph by R.A. Whitfield courtesy Rail Photoprints.

Above NO. 45558 – LEEDS

A trans-Pennine express moves away from Leeds behind no. 45558 *Manitoba* in 1962. Under BR, the engine was mainly at Patricroft shed, Manchester, though had four months at Leeds Holbeck in 1964, whilst no. 45558 was briefly at Newton Heath then being condemned. Photograph by Jim Carter courtesy Rail Photoprints.

Opposite above NO. 45557 – CHINLEY

In the early 20th century the London & North Western Railway and Midland Railway companies competed for traffic on the Manchester to London routes, with both being the same length. The MR faced the greater challenge to reducing and keeping time owing to the severe gradients through the Peak District. After Grouping the trains on the MR line were named the 'Peak Express' and the 'Palatine'. Following the Second World War, the first mentioned was lost while the 'Palatine' returned to use in 1957. This was attached to the 07.55 St Pancras-Manchester train, though later moved to 20.05, with the reverse starting off at 14.25 for arrival in London at 18.10. No. 45557 *New Brunswick* has the southbound train at Chinley, c. 1960. Photograph by Alan H. Bryant A.R.P.S. courtesy Rail Photoprints.

Opposite below NO. 45557 – NOTTINGHAM VICTORIA STATION

In late 1961 no. 45557 *New Brunswick* was amongst 17 class members allocated to Burton-on-Trent. These engines found use on the cross-country Sheffield-Bristol trains, in addition to Blackpool excursions. No. 45557 is at Nottingham Victoria station on 2nd March 1963. The engine was at Burton to June 1964 and had three months at Derby before sent to be scrapped. Photograph by Bill Reed.

Above NO. 45560 – HARTFORD

No. 45560 *Prince Edward Island* has a southbound freight train at Hartford during March 1963. The engine worked at Crewe North from June 1961 and was removed from traffic there in November 1963. Photograph by Colin Whitfield courtesy Rail Photoprints.

Opposite above NO. 45559 – BLACKPOOL CENTRAL STATION

Many seaside resorts across the country owed their existence and prosperity to the railways. Blackpool was no exception and developed from a place where the wealthy took a seawater cure to a holiday destination for the industrial workers in the North West. The Preston & Wyre Joint Railway branched to Blackpool in 1845, at which time the population was around 2,500, though by the end of the century had reached 35,000, with visitors numbering approximately 3,000,000. Both Blackpool and Lytham were reached by branches, yet in the early 1860s a connection between the two was thought desirable. This was completed with Hounds Hill the terminus in Blackpool. In the next decade, the station was connected to the wider network and renamed Blackpool Central. At the turn of the century significant expansion saw 14 platforms in use. No. 45559 *British Columbia* has an express there in 1961. The locomotive was allocated locally from July 1960 to October 1962 when condemned. To the right is Stanier 3P 2-6-2T no. 40164. Blackpool Central was closed in 1964 and the land was subsequently redeveloped. Photograph by Alan H. Bryant A.R.P.S. courtesy Rail Photoprints.

Opposite below NO. 45561 – CHESTER

No. 45561 *Saskatchewan* leaves Chester with an express for the North Wales Coast in 1949. The locomotive's front number plate now carries the BR identifier, yet is in the original scroll style rather than the later Gill Sans. No. 45561 is also decorated in the 1946 lined black livery. Both of these changes were made in May 1948. Photograph courtesy Rail Photoprints.

Above NO. 45562 – BARNSLEY STATION

For over 25 years, no. 45562 *Alberta* was at Leeds Holbeck shed. From there, around 20 class members had a wide sphere of operations. In 1964, no. 45562 relocated to Farnley Junction where the roles for Jubilees were limited. The main ones took locomotives to Liverpool, Manchester and York on expresses, whilst empty stock, shunting and banking duties were also undertaken. An unidentified working has taken no. 45562 to Barnsley station in 1966. In November of that year, the locomotive returned to Leeds Holbeck for the last 12 months in service. Photograph by P.C. Wakefield courtesy Colour-Rail.

Opposite above NO. 45562 – BRADFORD EXCHANGE STATION

On 7th October 1967 two of the surviving Jubilee Class locomotives were employed on 'The South Yorkshireman' railtour. No. 45562 *Alberta* started the day at Bradford Exchange station and crossed the Pennines to Manchester, then heading northward for Carlisle. Returning via the Settle & Carlisle line to Leeds, no. 45562 handed over to no. 45593 *Kolhapur* which took the party back to Bradford. The latter was condemned soon after the railtour and subsequently preserved, whereas no. 45562 went to the scrapyard in early November despite being the last class member in service. Photograph by Bill Reed.

Opposite below NO. 45563 – CARNFORTH

The 18.00 Warrington Bank Quay to Carlisle express has reached Carnforth behind no. 45563 *Australia* during July 1965. The locomotive's career came to an end in November and for the preceding two years had worked from Warrington. Photograph by Dave Cobbe courtesy Rail Photoprints.

Above NO. 45566 – KENTISH TOWN SHED

Initially, the Midland Railway was obliged to reach London through the courtesy of other companies. Firstly, an agreement was reached with the London & Birmingham Railway, then when this soured, the Great Northern Railway. Traffic volume on the latter soon led the MR to build a new line to the capital and this reached completion in the late 1860s. At the same time a major depot was provided at the London end – Kentish Town. The site (on the eastern side of the main line) accommodated a pair of roundhouses with extensive facilities. By the turn of the century major upgrades had been completed and three roundhouses provided stabling. These remained in use to the end of steam there during early 1963. From the mid-1930s, Jubilee Class locomotives were used at Kentish Town on the main line expresses. No. 45566 *Queensland* was not on the roster at the shed, rather the engine has arrived for servicing on 14th June 1962. Over a number of years, Leeds Holbeck had the locomotive's allocation. In the background, the Kentish Town mechanical coaler can be glimpsed which dated from just before the Second World War. Photograph courtesy Rail-Online.

Opposite NO. 45563 – CHESTER

In the early 1960s, Warrington began receiving Jubilee Class locomotives, numbering in the mid-teens to the end of 1965. No. 45563 *Australia* arrived there in late 1963 and remained to withdrawal. At the depot, the engines mainly travelled with freight to points in the area, as well as further afield, such as March, Cambridgeshire. No. 45563 has reached Chester here with an express freight during August 1965. The train is likely destined for Wrexham. The nameplate has been removed and little of the livery is visible, apart from a section of green on the cab side with the yellow diagonal stripe present, denoting the restriction from working on the main line south of Crewe. Photograph by Keith Langston courtesy Rail Photoprints.

Above NO. 45567 – GLOUCESTER
No. 45567 *South Australia* has been caught at Gloucester in 1965. Photograph courtesy Colour-Rail.

Opposite NO. 45573 – CARLISLE STATION
Despite the wet conditions, enthusiasts admire no. 45573 *Newfoundland* at Carlisle on 10th July 1965. Photograph by
D. Forsyth courtesy Colour-Rail.

Above NO. 45574 – WINWICK

Just north of Warrington at Winwick during 1962, a northbound passenger train approaches behind no. 45574 *India*. Winwick was the location for the junction for the loop to Wigan, whilst further along the main line was Vulcan Foundry before meeting the Liverpool & Manchester Railway. No. 45574 was a Blackpool engine when pictured and went on to have spells at Carlisle Kingmoor and Leeds Holbeck before condemned in March 1966. Photograph by Jim Carter courtesy Rail Photoprints.

NO. 45577 – BUILTH ROAD (HIGH LEVEL) STATION

Below

The London & North Western Railway held a dominant position between London, Manchester and Liverpool by the late 1840s and subsequently further solidified this by expansion. With the company's proximity to Wales and competition with the Great Western Railway, lines to the principal places in the country were desirable. First, the North Wales Line to Holyhead was taken over, then in the 1860s the LNWR backed several schemes that reached across Wales to Swansea. This became known as the 'Heart of Wales' line, whilst a similar project from north to south came to fruition around the same time. The two lines met just north of Builth Wells. Builth Road station opened on the Central Wales Extension Railway's line during 1866. In the late 1880s, the suffixes High Level and Low Level were given to the two stations on the respective routes. In late 1961, a number of Jubilee Class engines were allocated to Shrewsbury where a varied career awaited them. In addition to ordinary duties in the area, the locomotives could be seen in the West Country, on the South Coast and around South Wales, which was mainly reached via the 'Heart of Wales' line. No. 45577 *Bengal* is Shrewsbury-bound at Builth Road (High Level) station with the 09.45 train from Swansea Victoria on 20th May 1964. The engine was at Shrewsbury from September 1961 to September 1964 when withdrawn. Photograph by Hugh Ballantyne courtesy Rail Photoprints.

Above NO. 45578 – CREWE SOUTH SHED

Though allocated to Crewe North shed – the '5A' code is on the smokebox door – no. 45578 *United Provinces* is at Crewe South shed in the early 1960s. The depot was located amidst the running lines at the south end of Crewe station and offered an alternative location for servicing at busy periods. The locomotive had several allocations to Crewe North over the years and in the early 1960s this covered the period June 1961 to January 1962. Leaving for Aston shed, no. 45578 later moved on to Newton Heath and was condemned there in May 1964. Photograph by Bill Reed.

Opposite above NO. 45573 – KETTERING SHED

Following the experimental grey and 1946 livery applications, no. 45573 *Newfoundland* finally took BR green in December 1951. This was present to withdrawal in September 1965 and is still relatively bright here at the start of the year. The locomotive also has the yellow restriction stripe extending across to the edges of the side sheets. At Kettering shed, the engine was a long-term Leeds Holbeck resident. Photograph by Neville Simms from the Ranwell Collection courtesy Rail Photoprints.

Opposite below NO. 45577 – CREWE WORKS

This image shows no. 45577 *Bengal* under steam test in the yard at Crewe Works around late 1961. Also of note is the locomotive's number applied to the majority of components to ensure they returned for reassembly. Perhaps interestingly, the number is mostly the LMSR one rather than the BR number. No. 45577 transferred from Bristol to Shrewsbury when returned to traffic and continued in service to September 1964. The recorded mileage to early 1962 was 1.4 million. Photograph courtesy Rail Photoprints.

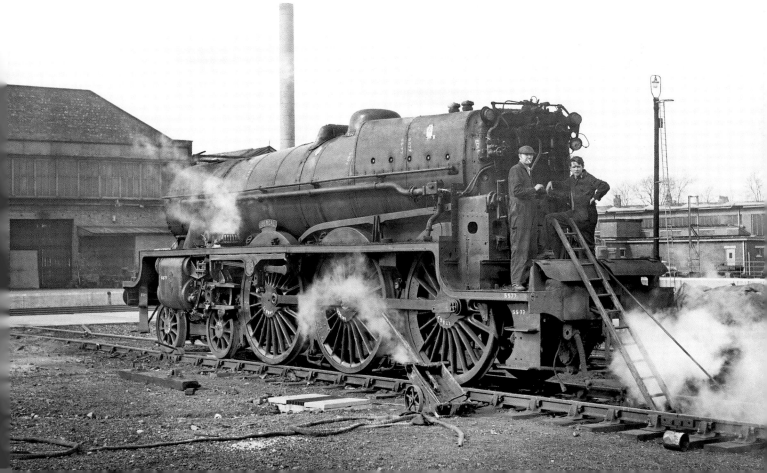

Above NO. 45581 – NEW BASFORD, NOTTINGHAM

View south from Perry Road, New Basford, Nottingham, to the ex-Great Central Railway main line which has no. 45581 *Bihar and Orissa* running light engine around 1964. In the background is New Basford carriage sidings. Photograph by Bill Reed.

Opposite above NO. 45582 – CARLISLE KINGMOOR SHED

'Not to be Moved' in the yard at Carlisle Kingmoor shed on 6th April 1959 is no. 45582 *Central Provinces*. The engine had worked northward from Preston. Photograph by Bill Reed.

Opposite below NO. 45583 – PATRICROFT SHED

Very well-presented no. 45583 *Assam* is on the turntable at Patricroft shed during May 1961. Photograph by Jim Carter courtesy Rail Photoprints.

NO. 45586 – RUNCORN

With 'British Railways' on the tender, no. 45586 *Mysore* has a southbound express at Runcorn during 1949. Photograph by R.A. Whitfield courtesy Rail Photoprints.

Above **NO. 45585 – DERBY**

The turntable belonging to the old North Staffordshire Railway engine shed at Derby is used by no. 45585 *Hyderabad* in September 1963. In the background on the left is Derby no. 4 shed. Photograph courtesy Rail Photoprints.

Below **NO. 45588 – CASTLE DOUGLAS STATION**

No. 45588 *Kashmir* stands at the head of the Scottish Rambler No. 2 railtour on 14th April 1963. One of more than a dozen locomotives used, no. 45588 led the party from Carlisle to Dumfries, then Castle Douglas where the reins were handed to Standard Class 4 2-6-4T no. 80023. Photograph courtesy Rail Photoprints.

Below NO. 45589 – BRISTOL BARROW ROAD

Passing Bristol Barrow Road engine shed, no. 45589 *Gwalior* has an express on 18th April 1963. Amongst the many duties for Leeds Holbeck engines were services to Bristol. No. 45589 arrived there in late 1950 and remained to June 1964. After nine months at Wakefield, the locomotive was condemned. Photograph by G. Parry courtesy Colour-Rail.

Above NO. 45590 – DERBY MIDLAND STATION

A southbound express, with at least one portion for Bristol (on the leading carriage headboard) has made a stop at Derby Midland station on 13th May 1956. The engine leading the train is no. 45590 *Travancore* of Sheffield Millhouses depot. A number of Jubilees were allocated there and other destinations served included Bath, Leeds and St Pancras. No. 45590 started work there in April 1951 and left at the end of December 1961. Derby station recently had 'Midland' added to the name in 1950, even though the Great Northern Railway's Derby Friargate had the distinguishing suffix added from the early 1880s. When the latter closed, Derby Midland reverted to Derby in 1968. The new concrete awnings installed during the modernisations of the mid-1950s are visible. Photograph by Bill Reed.

Above NO. 45592 – MANCHESTER VICTORIA STATION

Around 1962, no. 45592 *Indore* has an express at Manchester Victoria station. Apart from a short loan to Bushbury, the locomotive was at Carnforth from January 1960 to June 1964 when taken on at Newton Heath. Withdrawal occurred three months later. Approaching in the distance is Stanier Class 5 no. 45156 *Ayrshire Yeomanry*. The engine was in a minority of just five class members which were named. Photograph by Alan H. Bryant A.R.P.S. courtesy Rail Photoprints.

Opposite above NO. 45591 – CREWE WORKS

Apparently wearing an undercoat, no. 45591 *Udaipur* has likely completed a general repair at Crewe Works and is ready to be admitted to the Paint Shop for the full BR livery to be applied. This was finally determined in early August 1949, first appearing on no. 45566 *Queensland* and no. 45615 *Malay States*. Brunswick green was the colour with orange and black lining. The task to transform the class from the post-war black took several years and while the majority were in green from 1953, the last two finally took green livery in 1955 – no. 45574 *India* and no. 45656 *Cochrane*. Photograph by Bill Reed.

Opposite below NO. 45593 – BLACKPOOL CENTRAL SHED

No. 45593 *Kolhapur* had recently moved to Patricroft when pictured at Blackpool Central shed in October 1964. Moving northward from Burton, the engine had just three months there before a transfer to Newton Heath occurred. Two months later, no. 45593 was at Holbeck for the final seven months in traffic. Photograph by Bill Reed.

Above NO. 45595 – PATRICROFT SHED

All smiles as no. 45595 *Southern Rhodesia* has the smokebox cleaned in the yard at Patricroft during the 1960s. The engine was likely Crewe-allocated at this time. Photograph courtesy Rail-Online.

Above NO. 45598 – DUDLEY STATION
A special for Dudley Zoo has reached Dudley station with no. 45598 *Basutoland* in the early 1960s. Photograph by Bill Reed.

Below NO. 45598 – BAILRIGG
No. 45598 *Basutoland* is southbound at Bailrigg (south of Lancaster) with an express in November 1962. The locomotive's livery gleams in the winter sun and the BR green was first applied to no. 45598 in August 1950, whilst the second emblem was on the tender during April 1957, which made *Basutoland* one of the first Jubilee Class recipients. Photograph by Dave Cobbe courtesy Rail Photoprints.

Above NO. 45599 – RUGBY SHED

Extensive stabling facilities for locomotives were constructed by the LNWR on land just to the north of Rugby station. No. 45599 *Bechuanaland* is in this area here c. 1960. With '1A' on the smokebox door, the engine was allocated to Willesden which covered the period November 1959 to January 1961. At this date, the engine moved to Rugby and worked there to November when transferred to Nuneaton. A three-month loan brought the locomotive back to Rugby in February 1963. Withdrawal from Nuneaton took place in August 1964. Photograph by Bill Reed.

Opposite above NO. 45602 – LEICESTER LONDON ROAD STATION

No. 45602 *British Honduras* has a Manchester to St Pancras express at Leicester London Road station on 9th July 1957. On the right, a BR Standard Class 2-10-0 is with BR Class 11 shunter no. 12055. Photograph by D.C. Ovenden courtesy Colour-Rail.

Opposite below NO. 45603 – LICHFIELD TRENT VALLEY (LOW LEVEL) STATION

The order for Jubilee locomotives from the North British Locomotive Company was placed on the understanding of a quick turnaround. In the event, the delivery expected in the summer of 1934, turned into late 1934 and early 1935. Then, there were discrepancies between the date the NBLC thought the locomotive was ready compared to that the LMSR recorded. This gap for the final engines was particularly wide, with no. 45603 *Solomon Islands* having the longest at 111 days – 26th January 1935 for the NBLC, compared with 17th May 1935 for the LMSR. No. 45603 is at Lichfield Trent Valley (Low Level) station with a northbound freight on 4th June 1962. The engine was in service for just another six months before condemned. Photograph by B.W.L. Brooksbank.

Above NO. 45605 – NEWCASTLE CENTRAL STATION

Around 1960, no. 45605 *Cyprus* leaves Newcastle Central station with a southbound express. The locomotive was based at Leeds Holbeck, arriving there in April 1940 and employed to February 1964 when briefly relocated to Burton-on-Trent. Withdrawal occurred just a week later. Photograph by John Arnott-Brown courtesy A1 Steam Trust.

Opposite above NO. 45604 – ECCLES

Eccles station sits above the running lines in the background here as no. 45604 *Ceylon* moves westward with an express. The original station was built by the Liverpool & Manchester Railway in 1830 and later replaced. This second structure made way for modern facilities in the 1970s. Just to the west of Eccles was Patricroft Junction for Bury and Bolton. Photograph by Jim Carter courtesy Rail Photoprints.

Opposite below NO. 45606 – WEAVER JUNCTION

'British Railways' was an addition to no. 45606 *Falkland Islands'* tender in May 1948, whilst two months earlier, the 'M' prefix was added to the LMS cab number. The latter has changed in this image from 1949 to the BR number in 8 in. Gill Sans type. With the latter present, no. 45606 is seen post-May and has an express at Weaver Junction. During this period, and into the early 1950s, the locomotive was Willesden-allocated. Photograph by R.A. Whitfield courtesy Rail Photoprints.

Above NO. 45612 – SOULDROP

The 14.00 St Pancras to Bradford via Leeds is between Bedford and Wellingborough at Souldrop on 30th April 1955. This location had a prolonged incline northward towards Sharnbrook summit. For around three miles the ground rose at 1 in 119, reaching a high of 340 ft above sea level. Built as part of the Midland Railway's Hitchin Extension in the late 1850s, the route was soon found disadvantageous and in the 1880s some help was provided for freight trains. A new set of goods lines was laid and deviated just to the north west of Souldrop to run north-east to Wymington before rejoining the main line. This reduced the gradient to 1 in 200. No. 45612 *Jamaica* is the locomotive and was a resident of Kentish Town shed. A Fowler high-sided tender is coupled to the engine. Photograph by B.W.L. Brooksbank.

Opposite above NO. 45609 – DERBY SHED

A highlight in the railway calendar was often open days at British Railways' workshops. These not only promoted the company but raised money for railwaymen's charities. In the 1950s and 1960s, Derby Works opened the doors several times. On one occasion c. 1960, no. 45609 *Gilbert and Ellice Islands* was present at the nearby locomotive shed allowing a pair of young lads to experience the footplate of a Jubilee. The engine worked from Sheffield Millhouses throughout the 1950s and only survived until September 1960 when becoming the first non-accident related withdrawal of a Jubilee class member. Partially visible in front of the smokebox is the nameplate of no. 45561 *Saskatchewan*. Photograph by Bill Reed.

Opposite below NO. 45611 – CRICKLEWOOD

Raleigh bicycles employed several thousand people in Nottingham during the company's heyday in the 1950s. On a number of occasions, the workforce was transported away on excursions to various places in the country. In 1958 a pair of Nottingham's Jubilees have brought a company train to London and both are at Cricklewood here. In the lead is no. 45611 *Hong Kong* and behind stands no. 45650 *Blake*. Photograph by Bill Reed.

Above **NO. 45617 – ST PANCRAS STATION**
A trio of locomotives are together at St Pancras station during 1957. No. 45617 *Mauritius* is closest whilst the others are a Stanier Class 5 and Ivatt Class 4MT. No. 45617 was the first class member to have a Stanier 3,500-gallon tender from new though this has been replaced by the Fowler variety subsequently. Photograph by M. Beckett courtesy Colour-Rail.

Opposite above **NO. 45613 – HARTFORD**
Ten Jubilees entered traffic with a slightly different Fowler 3,500-gallon tender. These had side sheets that extended the full height of the coal space, whereas the others had coal rails. Another distinguishing feature was the width of the tender did not match that of the engine, leading to a noticeable gap between the pair. No. 45613 *Kenya* was built with the tender at Crewe Works in August 1934 and still carries the type here at Hartford on 21st June 1957. A partially-fitted freight train is behind the locomotive, which is travelling northwards. Photograph by B.W.L. Brooksbank.

Opposite below **NO. 45614 – ST PANCRAS STATION**
No. 45614 *Leeward Islands* was also amongst the batch of Jubilees coupled to a Fowler high-sided tender. Like with the other version, as mentioned, an attempt was made to change to the Stanier 4,000-gallon type. No. 45614 received tender no. 9780 in June 1940 following construction with a 4F Class 0-6-0. The locomotive has an express at St Pancras station on 18th March 1961. Photograph by B.W.L. Brooksbank.

Above NO. 45622 – RUGBY
A possible FA Cup final special is at Rugby on the ex-Great Central main line with no. 45622 *Nyasaland* on 25th May 1963. Leicester City was one of the teams contesting for the trophy, with Manchester United the other. Unhappily for Leicester fans, their team lost 3-1 in one of several final deafeats during the decade, yet a triumph came in 1964 as Leicester beat Stoke in the League Cup final. No. 45622 was Burton-on-Trent-allocated, arriving from Kentish Town two months earlier. Photograph by Neville Simms from the Ranwell Collection courtesy Rail Photoprints.

Opposite above NO. 45620 – DERBY
A southbound freight crosses the River Derwent led by no. 45620 *North Borneo* in June 1962. On the right is Derby Junction signal box which controlled traffic on the route to Chaddesden Sidings. Photograph courtesy Rail Photoprints.

Opposite below NO. 45620 – BURTON-ON-TRENT STATION
A goods train is heading through Burton-on-Trent station with no. 45620 *North Borneo* on 5th September 1962. In late 1961, the local depot received a number of class members. Photograph by B.W.L. Brooksbank.

Above NO. 45624 – NUNEATON

No. 45624 *St. Helena* has been captured on 31st July 1963 at Nuneaton. The engine was named in January 1936 and interestingly the full name of the island in the South Atlantic was not used on the nameplate – Saint Helena. This of course was the place where Napoleon was exiled following his defeat at Waterloo and the location of his death six years later. The same style of nameplate was used for another 'saint-named' locomotive, no. 45686 St. Vincent, though this was named after HMS *St Vincent*. No. 45624 was Nuneaton-allocated from November 1961 until condemned for scrap in November 1963. Photograph courtesy Colour-Rail.

Opposite above NO. 45621 – KILMARNOCK STATION

In Scotland, the Jubilees were mainly limited to Glasgow, particularly Corkerhill, though Polmadie had class members on occasion, as did Perth latterly, whilst Aberdeen had a few for just a short period in the late 1930s. No. 45621 *Northern Rhodesia*'s association with Scotland began in August 1952 when transferred to Corkerhill from Sheffield Millhouses. The engine went on to spend time at both Perth and Polmadie towards the end of the decade, then returning to Corkerhill. Withdrawal occurred in December 1962. At Kilmarnock station on 26th June 1961, no. 45621 has a parcels train. Photograph by Bill Reed.

Opposite below NO. 45623 – BIRMINGHAM NEW STREET STATION

Whilst the majority of Jubilee Class locomotives were repainted during the war to plain black, some managed to dodge the various Paint Shops to retain Crimson Lake throughout. No. 45623 *Palestine* was one such engine, though plain black was subsequently applied from mid-1948. At this time, the smokebox numberplate was upgraded to carry the additional '4' and the cab numerals fitted were of the smaller 8-in. variety. The tender had neither 'LMS' nor 'British Railways' and ran without identification. In April 1951, no. 45623 carried BR green livery with the first BR emblem. The locomotive is seen departing from Birmingham New Street station with an express on 16th June 1950. Photograph by Les Hanson from the David Hanson Archive courtesy Rail-Online.

NO. 45626 – CARLISLE STATION

No. 45626 *Seychelles* is at Carlisle station in 1964 with Ivatt Class 4MT 2-6-0 no. 43139. Photograph by P.C. Wakefield courtesy Colour-Rail.

Above NO. 45626 – DERBY SHED

A scene at Derby shed, captured on 12th June 1955. No. 45626 *Seychelles* stands at the turntable with Fowler Class 4P compound 4-4-0 no. 41094 and Thompson B1 Class 4-6-0 no. 61353. Photograph by Bill Reed.

Below NO. 45627 – BLACKPOOL CENTRAL SHED

On 18th October 1964, no. 45627 *Sierra Leone* stands in the yard at Blackpool Central shed. The locomotive was relatively local, working from Bank Hall depot between February 1962 and September 1966 when sent for scrap. Photograph by Bill Reed.

Below NO. 45630 – CREWE

An express freight approaches Crewe with no. 45630 *Swaziland* on 7th August 1958. Locally allocated, four months earlier the engine had been loaned to Liverpool Edge Hill briefly. No. 45630 remained employed at Crewe until withdrawn in November 1961. The locomotive was one of three to leave traffic during the year. Light engine in the background is Fowler 3F Class 0-6-0T no. 47414. Note the young lad getting a better view of proceedings in the top right. Photograph by S.D. Wainwright courtesy Rail Photoprints.

Above **NO. 45629 – WINWICK**

No. 45629 *Straits Settlements* pilots English Electric Type Four D214 *Antonia* with a southbound express at Winwick in October 1964. No. 45629 has acquired the yellow diagonal warning stripe on the cab side. This was applied at the start of September 1964 and signified running restrictions southward past Crewe owing to the danger posed by electrical overhead wires. Around 80 class members in service at the time were affected. Most stripes ran the full width of the cab-side sheets, whereas a variation existed with the line just painted within the lining. No. 45629 has the latter version here. The locomotive was also based at Carlisle Kingmoor. D214 was at Crewe but a short time later moved on to Camden. The diesel subsequently became BR Class 40 and renumbered 40014 in the 1970s and was scrapped in 1981. In the distance, Vulcan Foundry, which has 'Vulcan Locomotives' emblazoned on the factory roof, can be glimpsed. Photograph by Jim Carter courtesy Rail Photoprints.

Above NO. 45631 – RUGBY

Building speed away from Rugby, no. 45631 *Tanganyika* has an express around 1960. Another locomotive to keep Crimson Lake livery through the war years, no. 45631 subsequently received BR lined black in November 1948 with 'British Railways' on the tender. From September 1951, green adorned the locomotive and the colour is quite vibrant in this image. The second BR emblem has replaced the first, yet is the version which faced the wrong way. The grant of arms was given to face left. BR made an error by continuing to have the emblem facing to the head of the locomotive on both sides when on the right the lion looking to the train was correct. This oversight was later remedied, though was committed nationwide. Photograph by Bill Reed.

Opposite above NO. 45634 – CREWE NORTH SHED

Just to the north of Crewe station, on the west side of the line, stabling facilities for locomotives were established in the late 1830s. The site evolved over the years to consist of three large buildings, two for stabling and another for storing engines moving to and from the workshops. Around Nationalisation, the latter structure was demolished and replaced by a new semi-roundhouse building for the running department. Nestled in a corner of this shed during September 1960 is no. 45634 *Trinidad*. The engine was based at the depot several times under BR and was approaching the end of the last allocation here. Yet, following a brief spell at Willesden, the locomotive returned to Crewe, though at South shed. Crewe North saw steam end in May 1965 and the site has been redeveloped, now accommodating the station's car park, housing and retail premises. Photograph by Bill Reed.

Opposite below NO. 45634 – POLESWORTH

On the main line between Tamworth and Nuneaton, no. 45634 *Trinidad* has an express freight, with leading cattle wagons, at Polesworth on 3rd June 1955. Photograph by Bill Reed.

Above NO. 45638 – NOTTINGHAM VICTORIA STATION

The 08.38 express from London Marylebone is at Nottingham Victoria station on 12th October 1962. The locomotive is no. 45638 *Zanzibar*. Warrington-based at this time, the engine has perhaps connected to the train at Nottingham owing to the light engine headcode. In the late 1950s, the London Midland Region of BR took over the running of the ex-Great Central main line from the Eastern Region, increasing the instances of 'foreign' motive power. To the left of no. 45638 is a Thompson L1 Class 2-6-4T. Photograph by B.W.L. Brooksbank.

Opposite above NO. 45635 – WARRINGTON BANK QUAY STATION

Warrington's association with the railways began in the early 1830s as a mineral route connected with the Liverpool & Manchester Railway. This short line later became part of the larger Grand Junction Railway, as well as being part of the West Coast Main Line. In the 1850s, the St Helens Canal & Railway Company (from Garston Dock) met the Warrington & Stockport Railway at the south end of the town, crossing the main line. When both concerns were part of the LNWR, a connection between the two routes was promoted and Warrington Bank Quay (High Level and Low Level) opened in 1868. At the main line (High Level) station around 1964 is no. 45635 *Tobago* which is coupled to an express. Photograph courtesy Rail-Online.

Opposite below NO. 45636 – CHINLEY STATION

No. 45636 *Uganda* departs Chinley station with an express for the south in 1959. At this time, no. 45636 was Nottingham-allocated and would be to early 1960. The locomotive was mainly in the Midlands until condemned in December 1962. Photograph by Alan H. Bryant A.R.P.S. courtesy Rail Photoprints.

Above **NO. 45640 – HARTHOPE**

At Harthope, a Glasgow-express is dragged towards Beattock summit by no. 45640 *Frobisher* on 20th August 1955, with assistance provided at the rear. The engine was reaching the third anniversary of arriving for work at Carlisle Kingmoor, initially on loan, and remained there to the end in March 1964. Photograph by David Anderson courtesy Rail Photoprints.

Opposite **NO. 45639 – CREWE WORKS**

Decorated in plain black during the war, no. 45639 *Raleigh* had to wait until August 1954 when one of six to acquire BR green for the first time during the year. With those half-dozen Jubilees dealt with, just two remained to be repainted in 1955. No. 45639 is seen apparently well on the way towards completion of a general repair at Crewe Works, c. 1960. When re-united, the engine's tender should have borne BR's second crest which had been noted from at least the end of 1958. *Raleigh* had been amongst the Jubilees to have Sans Serif characters on the tender, taking this in early 1937. The engine also fell into the group of around 40-50 that had their tenders left without lettering or crests in the late 1940s. With a '55A' shed code on the smokebox door, no. 45639 would return for duty at Leeds Holbeck depot. The locomotive was allocated from July 1951 to September 1963 when condemned. Originally part of the London Midland Region, Leeds Holbeck was taken into the Eastern Region during 1957. Photograph by Bill Reed.

Below NO. 45643 – LEICESTER CENTRAL STATION

In the early 20th century, the Great Central Railway developed a Manchester-Bournemouth service, then under the London & North Eastern Railway further expansion of the train took place. Several portions, including ones from Newcastle, York, Bradford/ Leeds, were assembled at Nottingham to continue southward to Bournemouth.   After the war, the train was limited to Newcastle-Bournemouth, yet a Bradford/Leeds to Bournemouth was introduced subsequently.   On 18th July 1964, the 08.55 Bournemouth West to Leeds has reached Leicester with no. 45643 *Rodney*. At this time the engine was in the middle of an allocation to Farnley Junction and following three months at Leeds Holbeck, no. 45643 was withdrawn in January 1966. Photograph by Tony Cooke courtesy Colour-Rail.

Above **NO. 45642 – LUNE GORGE**

From Tebay to Beck Foot, the West Coast Main Line followed the River Lune before diverting off to the west, meeting Kendal, Oxenholme, etc. No. 45642 *Boscawen* has been caught on the aforementioned section in the early 1950s with an express. The locomotive was the first Jubilee, no. 5552, before the exchange of identities took place in 1935. Between this time and the early 1950s, the original Fowler 3,500-gallon tender was switched for the Stanier 3,500-gallon type and around this period another upgrade to the 4,000-gallon version occurred. No. 45642 worked from Newton Heath shed from May 1940 to withdrawal in January 1965. Photograph courtesy Rail Photoprints.

NO. 45648 – GLOUCESTER

On 20th October 1962, a northbound express leaves Gloucester with no. 45648 *Wemyss*. Photograph by Neville Simms from the Ranwell Collection courtesy Rail Photoprints.

Above NO. 45647 – CREWE STATION

The Saturdays-only 10.10 express from Edinburgh Princes Street to Birmingham New Street pauses at Crewe station on 22nd July 1961. No. 45647 *Sturdee* is at the head of the train, whilst to the right two locomotives, including Stanier 5MT 2-6-0 no. 42954, prepare to depart for servicing at Crewe North. Photograph by B.W.L. Brooksbank.

Below NO. 45647 – MANCHESTER EXCHANGE STATION

In the early 1960s, no. 45647 *Sturdee* draws a train away from Manchester Exchange station. Photograph courtesy Rail-Online.

Below NO. 45650 – STAMFORD TOWN STATION
The 12.10 Peterborough to Leicester service has reached Stamford Town station with no. 45650 *Blake* on 22nd June 1960. The Syston & Peterborough Railway opened throughout in May 1848 and linked the Midland Counties Railway with the Eastern Counties Railway at Peterborough. Stamford station served the local community from this time, but was later joined by one serving the branch to the Great Northern Railway's main line. Following Nationalisation, the two were differentiated by renaming, with the first becoming Stamford Town and the latter Stamford East. No. 45650 had joined the ranks at Leicester shed from Nottingham six months earlier and went on to enjoy 22 months' employment. Photograph by D.C. Ovenden courtesy Colour-Rail.

Above NO. 45651 – CHESTERFIELD

A short distance north of Chesterfield, the main line split as the original North Midland Railway line to Leeds continued northwards and the branch to Sheffield forged westward. Therefore, the junction was a busy section. No. 45651 *Shovell* has the 16.45 express from Bradford Forster Square to Bristol travelling southward, whilst two freight trains are heading northward, with the nearest consisting or iron ore. The image dates from 13th June 1957 and no. 45651 was employed at the Bristol end of the route, yet had spent 14 years at Leeds Holbeck previously. In late 1962, the engine was condemned at Shrewsbury after a year there. Photograph by B.W.L. Brooksbank.

Above **NO. 45653 – NOTTINGHAM VICTORIA STATION**
A parcels train is at Nottingham Victoria with no. 45653 *Barham* on 11th August 1963. Until a few months earlier, the locomotive was a long-term servant at Blackpool depot and had transferred to Saltley shed, Birmingham. In mid-1964, the engine briefly returned to Blackpool before having a year at Newton Heath until condemned in April 1965. Photograph by Bill Reed.

Opposite above **NO. 45654 – LIVERPOOL LIME STREET STATION**
With 33 Jubilees withdrawn during 1965, just 15 of the class remained in traffic. The Railway Correspondence & Travel Society organised a railtour to commemorate the class on 4th December 1965. Two trains ran and met at Manchester Exchange to cross the Pennines to Leeds and Yorkshire. One left Crewe, whilst the other departed Liverpool Lime Street station. The latter is about to get underway here behind no. 45654 *Hood*. The other Jubilee was no. 45596 *Bahamas* and the pair worked the main leg of the outing. Photograph by Colin Whitfield courtesy Rail Photoprints.

Opposite below **NO. 45655 – PONTEFRACT BAGHILL**
A southbound express passes Pontefract Baghill with no. 45655 *Keith* on 23rd July 1960. Photograph courtesy Rail Photoprints.

Above NO. 45658 – SHEFFIELD MIDLAND STATION

An unidentified express stands at Sheffield Midland station with no. 45658 *Keyes*. The locomotive was just one of two class members to have a solitary allocation over their careers. No. 45658 was associated with Leeds Holbeck from December 1934 to September 1965. Similarly impressive is the engine's recorded mileage up to September 1961 which stood at just over 1.7 million. All other Jubilee locomotives, apart from those rebuilt or withdrawn following accident damage, also ran more than one million miles in their careers. Photograph courtesy Rail Photoprints.

Opposite above NO. 45656 – MANCHESTER CENTRAL STATION

Underemployed on a local train to Chinley is no. 45656 *Cochrane* on 22nd December 1961. The locomotive was not a Manchester engine at this time, rather Sheffield Millhouses. Allocated there for the last decade, the depot closed at the end of 1961 and a transfer to Canklow occurred. In December 1962, no. 45656 was sent for scrap following six months at Darnall shed. Photograph by B.W.L. Brooksbank.

Opposite below NO. 45657 – GARSTANG & CATTERALL STATION

Around halfway on the line between Preston and Lancaster, Garstang & Catterall station was opened as Garstang on 26th June 1840 by the Lancaster & Preston Junction Railway. At the end of the decade, the Lancaster & Carlisle Railway took over operations and another ten years passed before the LNWR possessed both sections. The late 1870s saw the latter company rebuild Garstang following the opening of the branch to Pilling (later extended to Knott End) and in 1881 the station was renamed Garstang & Catterall. This was in use to closure in February 1969. A Windermere to Liverpool express is seen at the station on 30th July 1963 with no. 45657 *Tyrwhitt*. Photograph courtesy Rail-Online.

Opposite above **NO. 45661 – GREENHOLME**
A northbound express is at Greenholme, near the foot of the climb up to Shap summit on the WCML. For around five miles, the gradient rose at 1 in 75 to take the line 916 ft above sea level, which was the highest for the WCML in England. The climb for southbound trains was slightly longer but had a less severe gradient at 1 in 125. No. 45661 *Vernon* appears to be working the train easily without the aid of a banker in 1953. In the previous year, BR green had been applied for the first time, as well as the first BR emblem which is present here. Photograph courtesy Rail Photoprints.

Opposite below **NO. 45661 – HARTFORD JUNCTION**
The 12.15 Crewe to Blackpool passes Hartford Junction on 27th June 1964. No. 45661 *Vernon* leads the train past the connection with the Cheshire Lines Committee route from Northwich to Chester. The engine is travelling under the wires and gantries from the electrification project from Crewe to Liverpool completed in 1962. The connection to the Cheshire Lines Committee, just visible on the left, also has electrification lines. Photograph by B.W.L. Brooksbank.

Below **NO. 45660 – CHESTER**
In the Chester area on 22nd August 1964 is no. 45660 *Rooke*. The diagonal restriction stripe is prominent on the cab side and is the version which stretches through the lining to the edges of the side sheets. Also visible is the painted '6A' shed code on the smokebox door. This was for Chester and present over a two-month period when the engine was on loan there from Shrewsbury. No. 45660 likely did not return there as the following day a move to Leeds Holbeck shed occurred. Withdrawal was in late June 1966. Photograph by Bill Reed.

NO. 45663 – SHEFFIELD MIDLAND STATION
A southbound express starts away from Sheffield Midland station behind no. 45663 *Jarvis* in the mid-1950s. Photograph courtesy Rail Photoprints.

Above NO. 45662 – SHREWSBURY SHED

Work-worn no. 45662 *Kempenfelt* is between tasks at Shrewsbury shed in April 1962. Over six months earlier, the engine arrived from Bristol, ending an allocation lasting 14 years. No. 45662 only survived to the end of the year, though had amassed an impressive mileage – over 1.6 million. Photograph courtesy Rail Photoprints.

Below NO. 45664 – TROWELL

To the west of Nottingham, no. 45664 *Nelson* has an express at Trowell in June 1957. Throughout the 1950s, the locomotive worked from Sheffield Millhouses depot. Photograph by Bill Reed.

Above NO. 45670 – GLASGOW ST ENOCH STATION

A local service arrives at Glasgow St Enoch station with no. 45670 *Howard of Effingham* on 31st July 1961. Rugby-allocated, the engine has probably been pressed into service while in Glasgow. Photograph by D.J. Dippie.

Opposite above NO. 45668 – BROMFORD BRIDGE RACECOURSE STATION

No. 45668 *Madden* has been demoted to working a mixed mineral train on 5th September 1962. The engine is passing through Bromford Bridge Racecourse station which only opened for meetings and was to close just three years later. The land was subsequently reclaimed for housing, whilst the station was demolished. No. 45668 was a Burton engine when pictured and remained so until removed from traffic in December 1963. Photograph by B.W.L. Brooksbank.

Opposite below NO. 45669 – WILMSLOW STATION

On the line between Crewe and Stockport, Wilmslow station was electrified as part of the first scheme for the WCML to Manchester in 1959. The station dates from 1842 when opened as part of the Manchester & Birmingham Railway and later became the end of the Stockport avoiding line built in the early 20th century. No. 45669 *Fisher* has a short train stopped at Wilmslow in 1961. With '1A' on the smokebox door, the engine was Willesden-allocated which covered the period October 1959 to June 1961. At the latter date a move to Rugby ('2A') took place. Photograph by Alan H. Bryant A.R.P.S. courtesy Rail Photoprints.

Above NO. 45671 – CREWE WORKS

Amongst around 50 Jubilee Class locomotives to have the LMSR gloss black livery and lining was no. 45671 *Prince Rupert*. Nearly five years passed before the first application of BR green took place in early 1952. With the gloss black livery, the engine also had block-style cab numerals. No. 45671 is in front of the Paint Shop at Crewe Works, c. 1960, ready for a fresh application of BR green. Also in the yard is Fairburn 4P Class 2-6-4T no. 42674 and Ivatt Class 2MT 2-6-2T no. 41288. Photograph by Bill Reed.

Opposite above NO. 45672 – HEATON NORRIS JUNCTION

View north from Bowerfold Lane, Heaton Norris, as no. 45672 *Anson* passes Heaton Norris Junction with an express in the early to mid-1950s. The line curving off to the right is the Stockport to Stalybridge route which originally had a passenger service, though at this time had been discontinued. Photograph courtesy Rail-Online.

Opposite below NO. 45673 – DALMENY JUNCTION

At the southern end of the Forth Bridge, Dalmeny was the point where the line split three ways. One led westward to Linlithgow, Falkirk, etc. and two provided east/west connections to the Edinburgh-Glasgow main line. No. 45673 *Keppel* has been stopped by a signal at Dalmeny Junction and the driver is leaning out of the cab waiting for the change. The engine has a freight train on 29th May 1959. Photograph by David Anderson courtesy Rail Photoprints.

Above NO. 45675 – CREWE STATION

Crewe Works' Paint Shop has been busy rejuvenating the livery of no. 45675 *Hardy* during 1960. The date is likely around September when a speed indicator was fitted (coupled to the rear driving wheel) and before the addition of Automatic Warning System apparatus in 1961. The locomotive went from Crimson Lake livery to wartime black, then was a late recipient of BR green in late August 1954. For around a year, no. 45675 ran without tender branding until the first BR emblem was applied in June 1951, whilst the second (incorrect) version was used by mid-1958. No. 45675 is being run-in here, and the engine would be sent back to work at Leeds Holbeck. Photograph by Alan H. Bryant A.R.P.S. courtesy Rail Photoprints.

Opposite NO. 45674 – CREWE WORKS

No. 45674 *Duncan* appears to have missed the livery variants of the 1940s and was an early recipient of BR green. The colour was applied on the class from early August 1949, with no. 45674 being treated at the end of the month. At the same time, the first BR emblem was applied to the tender and was present for the next 12 years. The second crest was likely to appear on the tender following entry to Crewe Works' Paint Shop which is in the background here c. 1960. The engine returned to work at Crewe North and was a long-term servant, covering 22 years from 1941 to 1963. The locomotive's career ended at Saltley during October 1964. Photograph by Bill Reed.

Above NO. 45676 – GLOUCESTER EASTGATE STATION

The Midland Railway spread a tentacle out into the West Country thanks to the acquisition of two companies. These were the Birmingham & Gloucester Railway and the Bristol & Gloucester Railway. The latter opened in 1844, whilst the former was ready in 1840 and the MR bought the pair in 1845. The station at Gloucester was originally a terminus which required reversal and at the end of the century this difficulty was removed when a new facility was built a short distance away. This was renamed Gloucester Eastgate following Nationalisation to differentiate from the nearby GWR Gloucester Central. Initially in the London Midland Region, Eastgate was soon under the jurisdiction of the Western Region which later closed the station in 1975. During July 1963, no. 45676 *Codrington* is light engine at the station. For most of the year, the engine was Saltley-allocated. Photograph by J.L. Champion courtesy Colour-Rail.

Opposite NO. 45677 – BEATTOCK SUMMIT

No. 45677 *Beatty* is working with a reserve of steam at Beattock summit in 1955. The locomotive has a Manchester to Glasgow express consisting of seven coaches. Employed at Corkerhill depot at the time, this allocation began in August 1954 and lasted to the same month of 1959, when transferred northward to Perth. The engine later returned to Corkerhill in May 1960 and lasted to the end of 1962. No. 45677 had also spent two years at Polmadie shed earlier in the 1950s. Photograph by David Anderson courtesy Rail Photoprints.

NO. 45680 – GLASGOW POLMADIE SHED

Carlisle Kingmoor's no. 45680 *Camperdown* is at Glasgow Polmadie depot for servicing during August 1962. The engine left

...early in 1962. Photograph by D.J. Dippie.

Above NO. 45678 – WILLESDEN SHED

Standing in the yard at Willesden during 1958 is no. 45678 *De Robeck*. The engine was visiting for servicing and held two allocations during the year. For much of 1958, Crewe North had the locomotive, then a move to Liverpool Edge Hill occurred. Photograph courtesy Rail-Online.

Below NO. 45679 – PRESTON STATION

The 10.40 train from Blackpool North to Manchester Victoria arrives at Preston station with no. 45679 *Armada* on 8th September 1962. Originally built with a 4,000-gallon tender, the engine was elected to swap this for a Fowler tender with a Royal Scot, no. 6103 *Royal Scots Fusilier*, which occurred in 1937. Photograph by B.W.L. Brooksbank.

NO. 45682 – BATH GREEN PARK SHED

The Midland Railway's modest shed at Bath Green Park stands behind no. 45682 *Trafalgar* on 18th March 1964. Despite the small size, the depot was used to March 1966. Photograph courtesy Rail-Online.

Above NO. 45683 – BREDON

Between Worcester and Cheltenham at Bredon, no. 45683 *Hogue* works together with no. 45639 *Raleigh* to transport the 08.15 Newcastle to Cardiff service southward on 15th October 1960. Photograph by B.W.L. Brooksbank.

Below NO. 45683 – HARESFIELD

South of Gloucester, the 07.32 Bradford to Bristol express passes Haresfield on 29th July 1961. The locomotive is no. 45683 *Hogue*. Photograph by B.W.L. Brooksbank.

Above NO. 45685 – SHEFFIELD MIDLAND STATION

The driver of no. 45685 *Barfleur* takes time to smile for the camera as he departs from Sheffield Midland station with a northbound express in December 1963. Below him and above the running number is the power classification '6P'. Under the LMSR, this had been '5XP', yet was revised following Nationalisation and again in 1951 with regard to freight-haulage capabilities. This was downgraded to '5F' though this was not applied to the cab side and '6P' remained in use. No. 45685 had few allocations over 26 years in service and was based at Bristol when pictured and had been from November 1947. Withdrawal from there occurred in April 1964.

Opposite NO. 45686 – STOCKPORT STATION

Two named trains running between Manchester and London Euston were the 'Lancastrian' and the 'Mancunian'. Though in service for a number of years, the names were bestowed under the LMSR in the late 1920s. The trains ran opposite schedules, with the 'Mancunian' leaving Manchester London Road at 09.45 and travelling non-stop to Euston in 3 hours 35 minutes for the 188 miles. The morning train was particularly popular and a relief departed between 10 and 20 minutes later over the years, but running to Stockport and collecting 'through' coaches from several places in the area. This train also stopped at Macclesfield and Stoke-on-Trent before reaching London around 14.00. No. 45686 *St. Vincent* likely has this southbound relief 'Mancunian' at Stockport c. 1960. Photograph by Alan H. Bryant A.R.P.S. courtesy Rail Photoprints.

Opposite above **NO. 45688 – ASHCHURCH STATION**
The Boys' Brigade was founded in Glasgow during the early 1880s as a club to promote practical learning, activities and Christian values. In the mid-1920s, the Boys' Brigade merged with the Boys' Life Brigade and in recognition of this, the junior section of the club was renamed from the Boy Reserves to the Life Boys, which persisted until 1966. The Birmingham Area group of Life Boys has arranged an outing for members to the West Country here on 25th May 1957 and no. 45688 *Polyphemus* is at the head of their train. Photograph by B.W.L. Brooksbank.

Opposite below **NO. 45687 – CORKERHILL SHED**
After 1960, a high of over ten Jubilee Class locomotives was reached at Corkerhill shed. This was almost double the number previously working there. Yet, gainful employment was soon hard to find for them and many spent much of 1962 in storage. A pair was out of traffic at the start of the year, followed by half a dozen at the end of the summer season, then all in late 1962. A trio are seen awaiting disposal at the shed on 8th May 1963, with the leading locomotive being no. 45687 *Neptune*. Arriving at Corkerhill in August 1952 from Carlisle Upperby, withdrawal occurred during December 1962. Photograph by Bill Reed.

Below **NO. 45684 – GLOUCESTER**
Shunting a pair of vans in Gloucester on 16th June 1964 is no. 45684 *Jutland*. The engine was Derby-allocated for most of 1964, though towards the end of the year left for Bank Hall depot and was condemned there in December 1965. Photograph courtesy Rail-Online.

Above NO. 45690 – BRISTOL BARROW ROAD SHED

Two Jubilees are over the servicing pits at Bristol Barrow Road shed during 1962. The engine at the rear is unidentified, but the leading one is clearly no. 45690 *Leander*. The locomotive was condemned in 1964 and subsequently preserved. Photograph courtesy Rail Photoprints.

Opposite above NO. 45691 – STRANRAER

Historically, the main transfer of people, goods and animals between the north of Ireland and South West Scotland was made via Portpatrick. Yet, over time this port proved to be inadequate and other places were tried. North east of Portpatrick, Stranraer developed from the early 19th century and went on to dominate until the early 2010s when Cairnryan, further up the north-east coastline of Loch Ryan, was developed as the new port for ferry crossings. With a ferry on the left, no. 45691 *Orion* departs from Stranraer Harbour station on 28th July 1956. The station was opened by the Portpatrick Railway in October 1862, though was rebuilt in 1877. Despite the loss of ferry services, the facility – as Stranraer – continues to serve the local community. Photograph by N. Spinks courtesy Colour-Rail.

Opposite below NO. 45691 – HARTHOPE

No. 45691 *Orion* passes Harthope on the run up to Beattock summit. The engine has a relief express for Glasgow during July 1959. Photograph by David Anderson courtesy Rail Photoprints.

Above **NO. 45694 – LEA ROAD TROUGHS**
No. 45694 *Bellerophon* has the tender dramatically overfilling whilst taking water from Lea Road troughs on 9th July 1966. These were installed in 1885 between Lea Road and Salwick stations on the line from Preston to Blackpool/Fleetwood. The troughs remained in use for just under a year before closed. No. 45694 has a Sunday-only Blackpool to Bradford express. Photograph by Hugh Ballantyne courtesy Rail Photoprints.

Opposite above **NO. 45693 – BELLAHOUSTON**
The Glasgow & South Western Railway's line to Paisley became congested during the 1870s. To reduce the pressure on the route, the company turned to the Paisley Canal which the G&SWR had bought earlier. The canal was filled in and the course repurposed for rail lines. The junction for the new relief was made at Bellahouston, Glasgow, and reached Paisley, then rejoined the main line at Elderslie. A station was opened with the line at Bellahouston in 1885, though this closed for a time around 1920. Reopening later in the decade, the station continued to serve the area until 1954. In the early 20th century a carriage sidings was established on the west side of the station. No. 45693 *Agamemnon* passes through the remains of Bellahouston station with an express in the 1950s. Photograph courtesy Rail-Online.

Opposite below **NO. 45694 – KIRKHAM & WESHAM STATION**
A Blackpool Illuminations special passes Kirkham & Wesham station behind no. 45694 *Bellerophon* on 8th September 1962. The train is on the branch from the WCML at Preston which was originally built to serve Fleetwood in 1840 by the Preston & Wyre Railway & Dock Company. The rise of Blackpool as a resort subsequently reduced the importance of Fleetwood and a direct route there – the Marton Line – was laid at the turn of the century. No. 45694 had recently transferred from Leeds to Bradford Low Moor and the service had originated at the latter. Photograph by B.W.L. Brooksbank.

Above **NO. 45695 – LIVERPOOL EDGE HILL**
Filling much of the background is Edge Hill goods sidings which stored and sorted much of the traffic to/from Waterloo and Park Lane goods stations as well as Liverpool Docks. At the busiest periods, the yard could handle 2,000 wagons, with much of the shunting done by gravity. Passing by on 12th June 1959 is no. 45695 *Minotaur*. The locomotive has the 09.00 service from Hull via Leeds and Manchester. Photograph by B.W.L. Brooksbank.

Opposite above **NO. 45696 – DERBY SHED**
No. 45696 *Arethusa* received the BR numberplate in October 1948, as well as the cab-side number which is in the 'block' style. The Gill Sans number was present from December 1951, at which time the livery was upgraded to BR green. 'LMS' also likely disappeared from the tender at this time and the first BR emblem put in place. No. 45696 is in the yard at Derby shed on 10th September 1950. With a '17A' shed code on the smokebox door, the engine was on home ground and in the middle of a four-year allocation. In 1952, no. 45696 transferred northward to Glasgow Polmadie. Photograph by Bill Reed.

Opposite below **NO. 45697 – CARLISLE KINGMOOR SHED**
Involved in the exchange of tenders with the Royal Scot Class, no. 45697 *Achilles* received Fowler tender no. 4243 from no. 6158 *The Loyal Regiment*. Despite the schemes to upgrade these, no. 45697 remained with the type to withdrawal in September 1967. The engine is in the yard at Carlisle Kingmoor shed on 5th July 1961 when allocated there. No. 45697 celebrated 10 years at Carlisle in 1962, but moved on to Blackpool towards the end of the year. Photograph by Bill Reed.

Above NO. 45698 – SHAP

No. 45698 *Mars* was coupled to Fowler tender no. 4251 when entering traffic in April 1936. This had come from Royal Scot no. 6166 *London Rifle Brigade*. In March 1940, no. 45698 switched this with a Stanier 4,000-gallon tender built with a Fowler 4F Class 0-6-0. The type remains between engine and train here in July 1965 as the climb to Shap is undertaken without the aid of a banker. No. 45698 has the 13.10 Liverpool to Glasgow express. Photograph by Dave Cobbe courtesy Rail Photoprints.

Opposite NO. 45698 – YORK SHED

Surviving the war with Crimson Lake livery, in September 1947 no. 45698 *Mars* was repainted in the post-war black livery. The engine ran nearly five years with this until BR green was used from May 1952. In this period, no. 45698 went from 1948 to an undetermined date without branding on the tender, though the first emblem was likely applied with BR green in 1952. From just after Nationalisation in September, the locomotive was employed at Liverpool Bank Hall shed until condemned in October 1965. The locomotive is at York shed c. 1960, likely ready to return westward with a cross-country express. Photograph by Bill Reed.

Above NO. 45699 – DERBY

The 'Devonian' ran between Bradford Forster Square and Bristol Temple Meads with a 'through' portion for Torquay and Paignton. Operating for a number of years under the Midland Railway, the LMSR christened the train in 1927 and in the late 1930s accelerations made the service quite fast on the company's lines. Yet, following the Second World War the train suffered from the general lack of urgency and the journey was scheduled for nearly 10 hours both ways. Northbound, the train made several stops, with a mid-afternoon call at Derby. Spectators young and old witness the train passing on Five Arch Bridge, just north of the station crossing the River Derwent, behind no. 45699 *Galatea*, c. 1960. For most of the service's life, between Bristol and Leeds, the train was Jubilee-hauled. Photograph courtesy Rail-Online.

Opposite above NO. 45698 – WAKEFIELD KIRKGATE STATION

Rail enthusiasts from the North West belonging to the Stephenson Locomotive Society and Manchester Locomotive Society organised a tour of the Whitby area on 6th March 1965. Three locomotives were used. No. 45698 *Mars* brought the party from Manchester Victoria to Wakefield Kirkgate, then handing over to preserved Gresley K4 Class 2-6-0 no. 3442 *The Great Marquess*. Taking the train to Market Weighton, Peppercorn K1 Class 2-6-0 no. 62005 was paired with no. 3442 and the two engines worked northward to Filey, Scarborough and Whitby. The train returned southward via York and reached Wakefield Kirkgate to meet the waiting no. 45698. Photograph by L. Rowe courtesy Colour-Rail.

Opposite below NO. 45699 – YATE

No. 45699 *Galatea* again has the 'Devonian' train but in this instance is just north east of Bristol at Yate on 30th August 1959. The locomotive was allocated to Bristol at this time and had been from May 1948. No. 45699 had three years at Shrewsbury when transferred away from Bristol in September 1961. Photograph by Hugh Ballantyne courtesy Rail Photoprints.

Opposite above
NO. 45700 – GLASGOW CENTRAL STATION

In the late 1950s, a new scheme to reduce the number of Fowler tenders with Jubilees began with Stanier 8Fs donating their 4,000-gallon tenders. Around 40 locomotives were involved, including no. 45700 *Amethyst* in May 1959. Earlier in the decade, the engine had also switched names, originally being *Britannia*, though with the introduction of the Standard Class 7 Pacifics had to be renamed *Amethyst*. No. 45700 has the 10.55 Glasgow Central to Manchester Central express on 4th April 1961. Photograph by D.J. Dippie.

Opposite below NO. 45701 – SHAP WELLS

Passing Shap Wells (just south of the summit) with a northbound passenger train in the 1950s is Newton Heath's no. 45701 *Conqueror*. Received at the depot when new in April 1936, no. 45701's services were retained there until the engine was condemned in February 1963. Photograph courtesy Rail-Online.

Below NO. 45700 – GLASGOW POLMADIE SHED

The Caledonian Railway established Polmadie shed near Rutherglen station in 1875. Timber-built, the large 14-road depot amazingly survived to Grouping when the LMSR wisely rebuilt in brick. At this time a mechanical coaler with 400 tons capacity was installed, along with two 20,000-gallon water tanks. Around Nationalisation, further upgrades were made to the site, when another mechanical coaler with three bunkers was erected, in addition to an ash treatment plant. Both are in the background here as no. 45700 *Amethyst* is in the yard for servicing on 25th September 1955. Photograph by Bill Reed.

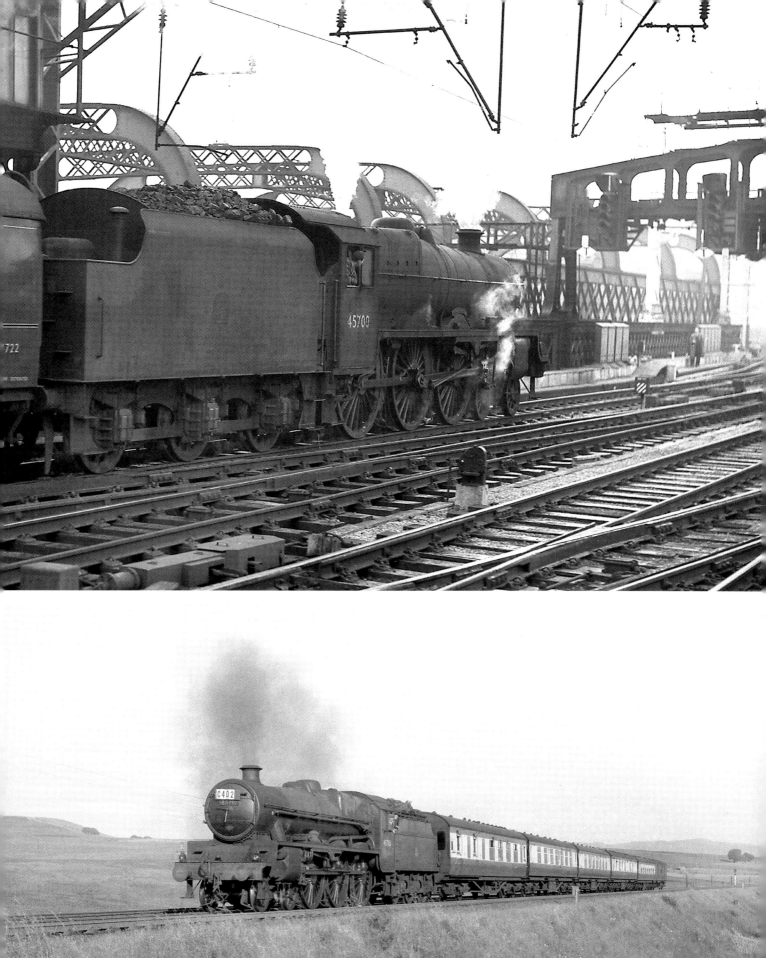

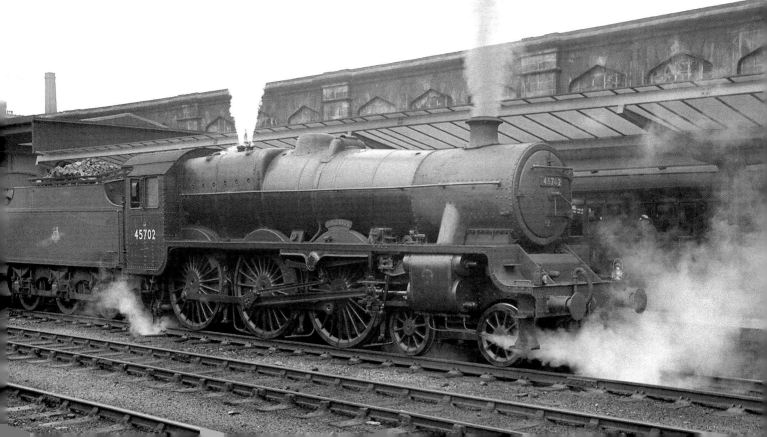

Above **NO. 45705 – MANCHESTER VICTORIA STATION**

An excursion train passes by Manchester Victoria station in 1960 with no. 45705 *Seahorse* at the head. The engine received a Stanier tender, no. 10758 from 8F no. 48733, in February 1959. Photograph by Alan H. Bryant A.R.P.S. courtesy Rail Photoprints.

Opposite above **NO. 45703 – CARPENDERS PARK**

Approaching Carpenders Park (just south of Watford) is the northbound 'Midlander' express led by no. 45703 *Thunderer* on 26th May 1953. The service was reintroduced in 1950, running between Euston-Coventry-Birmingham-Wolverhampton. The train north left London at 17.45 and due at Birmingham just over two hours later, with another 40 minutes onward to Wolverhampton. The reverse was a late morning departure for arrival in the capital around 13.30. Both Jubilees and Royal Scots were used on the service. Photograph from the Dave Cobbe Collection courtesy Rail Photoprints.

Opposite below **NO. 45702 – CARLISLE STATION**

BR no. 45702 was applied to *Colossus* from June 1948. This was the 'block' style before 8 in. Gill Sans numbers were applied from January 1950. Using a Fowler tender, this meant these were in line with the running plate and tender emblem. The latter was added in April 1951 and is apparently the middle size which was 15½ in. high, whereas Stanier tenders had the larger version 28 in. tall (a 9 in. version also existed). In the 1957 tender reallocation scheme, no. 45702 received no. 10248 from 8F no. 48521. This swap occurred in February 1959 which was six months after the locomotive was caught at Carlisle station on 8th August 1958. Photograph by D.J. Dippie.

Above **NO. 45704 – NEWTON-LE-WILLOWS**

In the Newton-le-Willows area, with a freight on the West Coast Main Line during April 1963, is no. 45704 *Leviathan*. The 1957 tender exchange programme had drawn to a close in 1960 with ten or so Jubilees still with Fowler tenders. As withdrawals took place, a small number of further exchanges occurred, yet engines still retained the Fowler tenders to the end. One of the last in service was no. 45704 which ran to withdrawal in January 1965. Despite not having a shed plate, Rugby's '2A' shed code has been painted on the smokebox door. In June, the locomotive was to make a final move on to Crewe North. Photograph by Colin Whitfield courtesy Rail Photoprints.

Opposite **NO. 45705 – HATCH END STATION**

On 27th June 1964, a special express travels northward through Hatch End station with no. 45705 *Seahorse*. The engine had just ended an association with the coast following a transfer from Blackpool to Newton Heath shed. No. 45705 had been in Blackpool from 1956 and for the 20 years before that was one of eight Jubilees new to Farnley Junction and one of six of these to spend multiple years at the depot. Withdrawal occurred in November 1965. Photograph by M. Stokes from the Keith Langston Collection courtesy Rail Photoprints.

Above NO. 45708 – MANCHESTER EXCHANGE STATION
A local train leaves Manchester Exchange station behind no. 45708 *Resolution*, c. 1960. The engine was employed at Farnley Junction, December 1944-February 1964. Photograph by Alan H. Bryant A.R.P.S. courtesy Rail Photoprints.

Below NO. 45710 – BLACKPOOL NORTH SHED
In 1963, a particularly well-presented no. 45710 *Irresistible* is in the yard at Blackpool North shed. The locomotive was based at Newton Heath from 1940 to withdrawal in June 1964. Photograph courtesy Rail Photoprints.

Above NO. 45709 – FENNY COMPTON

At Fenny Compton, the Midland Railway's acquired connection from the Bedford-Northampton line to Stratford-upon-Avon crossed the Great Western Railway's Leamington Spa-Banbury route. Saltley's no. 45709 *Implacable* is in the area with a loaded coal train on 5th October 1963. Photograph by Neville Simms from the Ranwell Collection courtesy Rail Photoprints.

Below NO. 45711 – HARTHOPE

Running at speed down from Beattock summit at Harthope, no. 45711 *Courageous* has a Glasgow-Liverpool/Manchester service on 19th April 1958. Photograph by David Anderson courtesy Rail Photoprints.

Opposite above **NO. 45716 – CARSTAIRS**
With much of the route northward from London to Scotland in place, a company was necessary to build the final section. This was the Caledonian Railway which obtained an Act of Parliament in 1845 to construct two lines from Glasgow and Edinburgh which met at Carstairs to continue onward to Carlisle – the authorised capital was nearly £2 million. The first part ready for trains was between Carlisle and Beattock in September 1847, followed by the line to Glasgow in February 1848 and Edinburgh in April. A southbound Glasgow to Carlisle local train has reached Carstairs with no. 45716 *Swiftsure* on 17th September 1956 and is passing under an impressive array of signals. Photograph by David Anderson courtesy Rail Photoprints.

Opposite below **NO. 45713 – GLASGOW POLMADIE SHED**
No. 45713 *Renown*'s career started in June 1936 at Camden but four months later the engine moved on to Farnley Junction. This proved brief as in November no. 45713 took a berth at Carlisle Kingmoor and remained there to July 1962. The engine was approaching the end of this here, being pictured in Glasgow Polmadie shed's yard on 15th August 1961. For the last three months in traffic, the locomotive was at Bank Hall shed. Photograph courtesy Rail-Online.

Below **NO. 45714 – PRESTON**
No. 45714 *Revenge* was in traffic from Crewe Works in July 1936. The engine was in the middle of a group of 23 locomotives that had a new boiler arrangement. The number of small boiler tubes increased to 159, in addition to the amount of elements rising to 24 with the same number of flue tubes. No. 45714 also had a second-hand Fowler tender provided from Royal Scot no. 6124 *London Scottish*. The locomotive is at Preston with a Manchester express on 25th November 1961. Photograph courtesy Rail Photoprints.

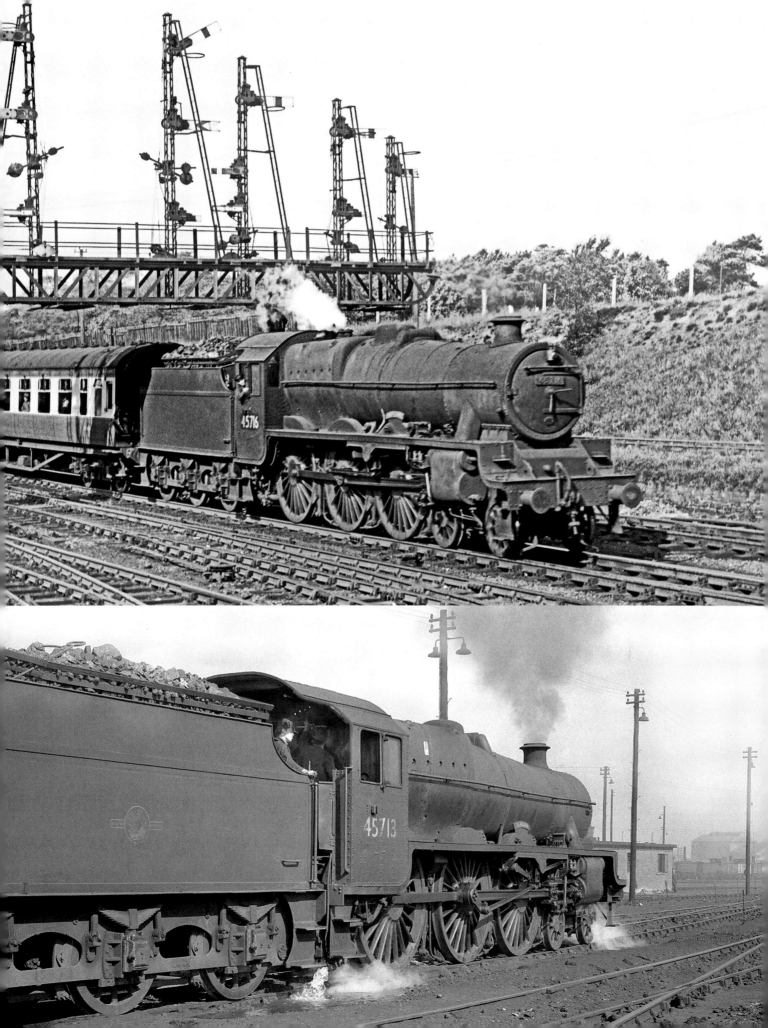

NO. 45717 – CREWE WORKS

No. 45717 *Dauntless* looks particularly fresh after a visit to Crewe Works c. 1960. Also present is War Department 'Austerity' 2-8-0 no. 90420. Photograph by Bill Reed.

NO. 45721 – CARLISLE STATION

A scene captured on 2nd July 1965 with no. 45721 *Impregnable* at Carlisle station. Photograph by D. Forsyth courtesy Colour-Rail.

Above NO. 45726 – BLETCHLEY

Being in close proximity to Crewe Works where many Jubilees were produced and repaired, Crewe shed saw many, if not all, class members over the years. Of those officially allocated, over three quarters of the class had spells there, with a high of over 50 in the mid- to late 1930s. Following Nationalisation, this had decreased significantly to 10-15 for a variety of duties on the routes radiating from Crewe. The jobs were mainly passenger trains but also included express freight diagrams. A particularly long example of the latter trails behind Crewe's no. 45726 *Vindictive* here at Bletchley on 27th July 1963. The engine had been at the depot first in 1949 for over eight months into 1950, later returning in 1953 for a decade, though broken by some loan spells. Moving on to Warrington, no. 45726 was condemned there in March 1965. Photograph by David Anderson courtesy Rail Photoprints.

Below NO. 45723 – RUGBY STATION

No. 45723 *Fearless* first had BR green livery from January 1952, though the first BR emblem had been present from late 1950. The Sans Serif numberplate was replaced shortly after Nationalisation, though the cab number style changed several years earlier. In 1960, the second BR crest was applied. The locomotive is at Rugby station on 17th August 1963 waiting to take over a southbound express to Euston. Based at the local shed, this was likely the location of the non-standard modification to the smokebox numberplate, with the corners and securing bolts painted white, in addition to part of the hinge straps and top handrail. Photograph by Neville Simms from the Ranwell Collection courtesy Rail Photoprints.

Above NO. 45728 – GLASGOW POLMADIE SHED

Resting in the yard at Glasgow Polmadie shed on 4th August 1961 is no. 45728 *Defiance*. The engine has the larger number on the cab side and should have the second BR emblem on the tender though this appears missing or is completely obscured by dirt and grime. The locomotive was shortly to end a long-standing association with Carlisle Kingmoor and defect over to Carlisle Upperby. Photograph by D.J. Dippie.

Opposite above NO. 45726 – PATRICROFT SHED

Situated between Eccles and Patricroft stations on the Liverpool & Manchester Railway line, Patricroft shed was bounded by Patricroft sidings, the Bolton-Wigan-Manchester route, the Clifton branch and sidings belonging to an engineering firm. Despite the restricted space, the LNWR was able to erect an eight-road building in 1885, followed by a ten-track structure in the early 20th century. The turntable was placed in the corner between the two buildings, which were at a right angle to each other. The 1885 structure is to the right and the 1904 one behind no. 45726 *Vindictive* which is on the turntable during 1962. By this time, the ten-road shed had been reduced to four when BR replaced the roof. Patricroft remained open to steam until July 1968 and was later demolished. Photograph courtesy Rail Photoprints.

Opposite below NO. 45727 – EDINBURGH WAVERLEY STATION

Perth's no. 45727 *Inflexible* has an express bound for the city at Edinburgh Waverley station on 1st June 1956. The engine had been in the Scottish Area from 1937 and remained so until condemned in December 1962. No. 45727 was allocated to Perth from early 1953 until the end of the decade when transferred to Corkerhill. Photograph from the Gordon Edgar Collection courtesy Rail Photoprints.

Above NO. 45729 – GLASGOW ST ENOCH STATION

An ambitious plan to link all the railway lines entering Glasgow was formulated by the City of Glasgow Union Railway in the early 1860s. This did not find favour with all companies, yet the project progressed to completion in 1870. A main feature of the scheme was a station at St Enoch Square, the construction of which took several years and did not welcome traffic until 1876. There were six platforms covered by a glass train shed 198 ft wide and 504 ft long. Subsequently, the Glasgow & South Western Railway took over St Enoch station and entered a partnership with the Midland Railway to accept trains from England. St Enoch was in use to 1966 and later demolished. No. 45729 *Furious* is departing with a local train on 21st April 1962. Photograph by D.J. Dippie.

Opposite NO. 45731 – HEST BANK STATION

A pair of Jubilees have an express freight southbound through Hest Bank station in June 1962. The station was to remain in use for just a short time as closure occurred in 1969. The Lancaster & Carlisle Railway opened the station – around three miles north of Lancaster – in 1846. No. 45731 *Perseverance* is piloting, whilst the train engine has gone unrecorded. The locomotive was Upperby-allocated but moved on to Kingmoor in July, soon followed by Blackpool. No. 45731 did not survive long there and was removed from service in October. Photograph by Dave Cobbe courtesy Rail Photoprints.

Above **NO. 45730 – NEWTON-LE-WILLOWS**

Another through freight is at Newton-le-Willows, c. 1963. The engine in this instance is no. 45730 *Ocean*. With '24L' on the smokebox door, the allocation was Carnforth which covered the period September 1961-June 1963. Following four months at Warrington subsequently, the locomotive was condemned and later scrapped at T.W. Ward's scrapyard, Beighton, Sheffield. Photograph by Colin Whitfield courtesy Rail Photoprints.

Opposite **NO. 45733 – PRESTON**

No. 45733 *Novelty* heads northward away from Preston with an express freight around 1960. The signal box standing behind the locomotive was amongst over 80 replaced when a power signal box was built at Preston in the early 1970s. Photograph courtesy Rail Photoprints.

Below NO. 45735 – BLETCHLEY

Stanier had little luck with his boiler design for the LMSR in his first years. Following the problems with the Jubilee Class, the high-pressure locomotive, no. 6399 *Fury*, was rebuilt as no. 6170 *British Legion* and found further steaming troubles. A serious redesign of the boiler was necessary but found success afterwards, leading to an experiment with two Jubilees and a similar boiler. This had a higher heating surface than the final Jubilee boiler with a working pressure 25 lb per sq. in. greater at 250 lb per sq. in. and a double chimney was provided. The pair proved their superiority to the standard Jubilees, but no further conversions occurred, though the boiler type did find use with Royal Scots and Patriots later. Nos 5735 *Comet* and 5736 *Phoenix* were the two Jubilees rebuilt in May and April 1942 respectively. On 31st March 1963, no. 45735 has a northbound express freight at Bletchley. On the left of the engine is Bletchley flyover which was erected in 1959 to carry the Oxford-Cambridge route over the WCML. Although the line was subsequently closed, a new scheme has seen the flyover replaced recently. Photograph by Neville Simms from the Ranwell Collection courtesy Rail Photoprints.

Above **NO. 45736 – BRISCO**

Just south of Carlisle at Brisco, no. 45736 *Phoenix* has a partially-fitted freight on 3rd July 1964. One of the final modifications made to the Jubilee Class was the relocation of the top lamp iron on the smokebox door to a position lower between the hinges in order to guard against electrocution when under the wires. The train is passing Brisco station which only opened for a few years following the completion of the Lancaster & Carlisle Railway in the late 1840s. Recently, the site has been cleared. Photograph by D. Forsyth courtesy Colour-Rail.

Above NO. 45738 – BUSHEY

On 23rd August 1952, no. 45738 *Samson* passes Bushey with a Euston to Wolverhampton express. The engine was based at the latter and had recently moved there from Camden. At the end of the decade, *Samson* went to Carlisle Upperby and also had a spell at Kingmoor before leaving service in December 1963. Photograph by C.R.L. Coles from the Dave Cobbe Collection courtesy Rail Photoprints.

Opposite NO. 45737 – ATHERSTONE STATION

Just three coaches form the 11.45 Liverpool to Rugby train which has made a stop at Atherstone station on 23rd May 1961. The locomotive is no. 45737 *Atlas* of Crewe which is still presentable following a repair earlier in the year. At this time the second BR crest was applied to the tender, in addition to a speed indicator being fitted on the driver's side. AWS equipment had been fixed to the bufferbeam at the previous general repair in late 1959. No. 45737 was at Crewe from June 1960 to March 1962 when making the final move to Newton Heath. The locomotive was condemned at the depot in May 1964. Atherstone sits to the north west of Nuneaton on the LNWR's Trent Valley line bypassing Birmingham. A station was provided in 1847 and built to the design of J.W. Livock. This was listed in 1980 and subsequently restored, having been unused for over a decade. At the present time, the building is used as a veterinary practice. Photograph by Hugh Ballantyne courtesy Rail Photoprints.

Below NO. 45740 – CREWE SOUTH SHED

No. 45740 *Munster* is in the yard at Crewe South shed before July 1960 when transferred away from Willesden depot, as the latter's '1A' code is still present on the smokebox door. The locomotive was the lowest-numbered Jubilee to be paired with a Fowler tender, taking no. 3926 from no. 6130 *The West Yorkshire Regiment* in late 1936. The new tender built with no. 45740 did not go to a Royal Scot, rather tender no. 9374 had a 10-ton capacity and went to Princess Royal Pacific no. 6203 *Princess Margaret Rose*. No. 45740 went on to receive a 4,000-gallon tender built with a Fowler 4F in July 1939 only to lose this to Patriot Class no. 5532 *Illustrious* in June 1948. Classmate no. 45739 lost a 4,000-gallon tender to no. 45740 in the 1957 programme. This occurred in February 1960. Photograph by Bill Reed.

Above NO. 45740 – HARROW AND WEALDSTONE STATION

An express freight passes Harrow and Wealdstone station with no. 45740 *Munster* post 1960. The engine is now running with a Stanier 4,000-gallon tender (see opposite). After leaving Willesden, no. 45740 was either at Crewe North or Llandudno Junction over a year before settling at Aston in September 1961. The locomotive left service from there in October 1963. Photograph by Bill Reed.

Above NO. 45742 – KILMARNOCK STATION

A southbound freight is at Kilmarnock station on 7th May 1963 with no. 45742 *Connaught*. Approaching a year's employment at Carlisle Kingmoor, the locomotive was there for another two years before sent to Motherwell Machinery & Scrap Co. The large Johnnie Walker whisky bottling plant can be seen in the background. This closed in 2012 and the site cleared for a college development. Photograph by Bill Reed.

Opposite above NO. 45741 – BIRMINGHAM NEW STREET STATION

No. 45741 *Leinster* was fitted with a speed indicator in October 1960, yet this is still to take place here. The locomotive is at Birmingham New Street station with Stanier 3MT 2-6-2T no. 40108 in the late 1950s. Photograph courtesy Rail Photoprints.

Opposite below NO. 45742 – CARLISLE KINGMOOR SHED

No. 45742 *Connaught* is serviced in the yard at Carlisle Kingmoor in July 1964. Photograph by Bill Reed.